Scotland's leading educational publishers

National 5
MODERN STUDIES
SUCCESS GUIDE

N5 MODERN STUDIES SUCCESS GUIDE

Patrick Carson

© 2019 Leckie & Leckie Ltd
Cover image © ink-tank and associates/Jane Rix

001/09012019

10 9 8 7 6 5 4 3 2 1

ISBN 9780008281755

Published by
Leckie & Leckie Ltd
An imprint of HarperCollinsPublishers
Westerhill Road, Bishopbriggs, Glasgow, G64 2QT
T: 0844 576 8126 F: 0844 576 8131
leckieandleckie@harpercollins.co.uk www.leckieandleckie.co.uk

Printed in Italy by Lego S.P.A.

A CIP Catalogue record for this book is available from the British Library.

Acknowledgements

We would like to thank the following for permission to reproduce their material:
Sources for exam-style questions © Scottish Qualifications Authority; Article on P23 used with permission from The Herald, © Newsquest Media Group; P23 Nicola Sturgeon image © Twocoms / Shutterstock.com; Jamie Oliver image © Fetureflash Photo Agency / Shutterstock.com; P25 © Zoran Karapancev / Shutterstock.com; P28 reproduced with the permission of Parliament; P34 © Lee Thomas / Alamy Stock Photo; P36 © Ken Jack / Alamy Stock Photo; P37 ©Ken Jack / Alamy Stock Photo; P40 © gerard ferry / Alamy Stock Photo; P51 © Peter Wheeler / Alamy Stock Photo; P62 © David Leveson / Alamy Stock Photo; P52a reproduced courtesy of Nicola Sturgeon; P67 © Newscom / Alamy Stock Photo; P70 © TonuV3112 / Shutterstock.com; P75 © Hung Chung Chih / Shutterstock.com; P84 © Federic Legrand – OMEO / Shutterstock. com; P87 © Tonis aling / Shutterstock.com; P88 © LINGTREN IMAGES / SHutterstock. com; P89 ©Agênica Brasil/Antônio Milena; P92 © Jeremy Richards / Shutterstock.com; P103 reproduced courtesy of the US Government; P105 ©Bettmann / Contributor / Getty Images ; P110 © BrandonKleinVideo / Shutterstock.com; P111 reproduced courtesy of the United States Senate; P114 © Tribune Content Agency LLC / Alamy Stock Photo

All other images from Shutterstock and Thinkstock.

Whilst every effort has been made to trace the copyright holders, in cases where this has been unsuccessful, or if any have inadvertently been overlooked, the Publishers would gladly receive any information enabling them to rectify any error or omission at the first opportunity.

To access the ebook version of this Success Guide visit
www.collins.co.uk/ebooks
and follow the step-by-step instructions.

Contents

The course and the assessment

Democracy in Scotland and the United Kingdom

Contents

International Issues - India

International Issues - The USA

Why should you study Modern Studies?

The aims of the course

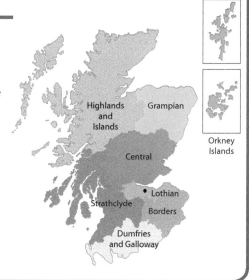

By studying Modern Studies you will develop your knowledge and understanding of recent and current issues affecting your local area, Scotland, the United Kingdom and the world. It will prepare you to become active citizens of Scotland, the United Kingdom, Europe and indeed the world beyond.

Skills

By studying Modern Studies you will also develop a set of highly transferable skills that will be important in your learning, life and work. These skills include the following:

- a wide range of information handling skills
- investigation skills – locating, selecting and presenting information
- the ability to use a range of sources of information to:
  - support and oppose views
  - give detailed justifications for decisions
  - give detailed support for valid conclusions
- the ability to think and work independently

Knowledge and understanding

The course will also develop your knowledge and understanding of current issues at a local, Scottish, UK and international level including:

- the democratic process
- social and economic issues
- how needs are met and how inequalities are addressed
- different views about how far the state should be involved in society

- the causes of and attempts to deal with conflict
- rights and responsibilities in different societies

Skills for learning, skills for life and skills for work

Studying Modern Studies will also develop skills that are important in life and work such as:

- literacy
- numeracy
- employability, enterprise and citizenship
- thinking skills

The course

The course consists of three areas of study. Within these areas of study you can choose topics. This book includes the following topics:

1. Political Issues – Democracy in Scotland and the United Kingdom.
2. Social Issues – Inequality in Scotland and the United Kingdom.
3. International Issues – India, China and the USA.

Assessment

There are two parts to the course assessment.

The assignment

There will be an assignment that involves an investigation. This investigation can be about any topic from the course and your teacher will give you reasonable assistance to help you choose. The assignment is worth 20 marks and is part of the course assessment. You can find more information about the assignment on page 18.

The exam

The exam consists of a single question paper lasting 2 hours and 20 minutes. It will assess your skills and breadth of knowledge and understanding across the three units of the course. The question paper will assess your ability to:

- make and justify decisions
- support and oppose views
- give detailed descriptions and explanations with some analysis
- draw and support conclusions

The question paper is worth 80 marks. There will be more marks available for knowledge and understanding questions of the "describe" and "explain" type than for the source based skills questions. It is divided into three sections, each covering one of the areas of study – Political Issues, Social Issues and International Issues. Each section will have two options to choose from and each will have questions worth between 4–10 marks.

The options you can choose from in each Section are as follows:

Section 1: Democracy in Scotland and the United Kingdom you can choose from:Democracy in Scotland or Democracy in the United Kingdom

Section 2: Social Issues in the United Kingdom you can choose from Social Inequality or Crime and the Law

Section 3: International Issues you can choose from World Powers or World Issues

Skills and knowledge

Knowledge and understanding questions

In the National 5 Modern Studies exam, you will be expected to answer source-based skills questions (which are dealt with elsewhere in the book) and knowledge and understanding questions.

A knowledge and understanding question is about a lot more than just remembering facts – although these are important too! A knowledge and understanding question will test your understanding as well as your memory.

There are two types of knowledge and understanding question: describe and explain.

Describe questions

Here you will be expected to give detailed descriptions of an issue that draw on your factual knowledge. For example:

> *Describe* the different types of housing available to meet the needs of elderly people.

In this answer you might *describe* elderly people living in their own home, sheltered housing, very sheltered housing, nursing homes etc.

Explain questions

Here you should be able to make an issue plain or clear by, for example, showing connections between factors and/or between events and ideas. For example:

> *Explain* why some elderly people live in better housing than others.

In this answer you will be expected to give reasons for the differences. For example some elderly people have more money than others and can live in a better area, some might live with their family, some might live in houses that have been adapted to meet their needs – ramps, hand rails, stair lifts etc.

This is a bit like the difference between answering a 'what' question and a 'why' question.

Using PADRE

A good knowledge and understanding answer will do three things.

1. Make your **P**OINT.
2. Give **A**DDITIONAL **D**ETAIL.
3. Support your answer with **R**ELEVANT **E**XAMPLES.

If you use the starting letter of each of these important steps you come up with PADRE (Spanish for 'father').

P	OINT
A	DDITIONAL
D	ETAIL
R	ELEVANT
E	XAMPLE

> Describe the advantages of the First Past the Post voting system. (4 marks)

Here is a good answer to the question:

One advantage of the First Past the Post voting system is that it easy to understand (POINT). This means that the voter only has to mark an 'X' beside the name of the candidate they want to win and so they are less likely to make mistakes (ADDITIONAL DETAIL). For example, this system was used to elect Members of Parliament in the 2017 UK elections (RELEVANT EXAMPLE).

A second advantage of the First Past the Post voting system is that it usually produces a quick result (POINT). This means that there is very little time between the previous government leaving and the new government taking over (ADDITIONAL DETAIL). For example, in the 2017 UK election, the Conservative Party became the government the next day (although they had to rely on the support of the Democratic Unionist Party (DUP) to make up a majority in the House of Commons (RELEVANT EXAMPLE).

EXAM TIP

When you are including examples, try to make them fit 'the three Rs':
- Reliable (come from a trusted source)
- Recent
- Relevant

You should also notice that this question was worth 4 marks. You can be awarded up to three marks for each 'well made' PADRE point in a 'describe' question. Shorter points, if relevant, will still gain marks but not as many. To be safe you should try to make 2 separate points in a four mark answer, three in a six mark answer and so on.

Using flag words in 'explain' answers

You should use certain words to 'flag up' or show the examiner what you are doing in your explain type answer:

- when you are explaining: 'this means…' or 'what this means is…" This shows that you have analysed the situation you are referring to.
- when you are giving a relevant example: 'a good example of this would be when…' or more simply, "…for example."
- when you have moved on to make your second or third point: 'secondly…' or 'another way in which…'

Here is an example of a more challenging explain question using the flag words.

> Explain in detail why the Additional Member System could be considered a fairer system. (8 marks)

The first reason that the Additional Member System could be considered fairer is that it is more proportional. This means that the percentage of the seats that each party wins in the Scottish Parliament is more proportional. For example, in the Scottish election of 2016, The SNP won the largest percentage of the vote and the largest percentage of the seats.

A second reason that the Additional Member System could be considered fairer is that it keeps the link between individual constituencies and an MSP. What this means is that each constituency has a specific MSP to represent them in the Scottish Parliament. An example of this this is that Nicola Sturgeon, the First Minister is the MSP for Glasgow Southside.

Thirdly, the AMS system is fairer because it gives the voters more choice. If they wanted to, voters could vote for a particular party in their constituency but could choose to vote for a different party using their second Regional List vote.

First ➔ tells examiner there is more to come.

This means... ➔ flags up your explanation.

Second ➔ means, 'I have now moved on to my next point'.

However ➔ means, 'I have moved on to the disadvantages'.

Three Rs ➔ examples – recent, real, relevant.

Therefore ➔ another way of saying, 'this means...'

Remember that you can achieve up to 4 marks for a single explanation if it is accurate and developed with some analysis.

Layout – make your answers look structured. Miss a line and start a new paragraph every time you start a new PADRE point so that the examiner sees two separate sections for a 4-mark answer or three/four for an 8-mark answer, etc.

Supporting and opposing a point of view

In this type of question you will be given a statement or point of view and you must use a range of sources to support *and* oppose that point of view. As with all source-based questions in the National 5 exam, you will be expected to link different sources to 'prove' your point. This type of question, as with the other source-based questions, is worth 10 marks. You can be awarded up to three marks for each argument depending on the quality of your argument and the accurate use of sources to support it. All sources must be referred to at least once in your answer. Remember you MUST support AND oppose the viewpoint. Any answer that does not do both can only gain a maximum 6 marks.

Setting out your answer

It important as you prepare for the exam that you have practiced and can use a plan to answer each type of question, (remember the use of 'PADRE' to answer 'describe type' questions). When answering a support / oppose type questions your answer could be set out like this:

If the point of view was, for example:

> There is widespread support in Scotland for independence.
>
> **View of Clare Bradley**

you should set your answer out like this:

"I can support the view of Clare Bradley when she states 'There is widespread support in Scotland for independence' because Source … shows that (information from source) and this is backed up by source …. which shows that (information from a different source). Therefore, as the support for independence has been significant over the whole of the period shown in the sources since the referendum, this supports the view of Clare Bradly that there is still widespread support for independence in Scotland."

Using words and phrases such as "significant" and "over the whole of the period shown" shows the examiner that you have evaluated and not just repeated the sources.

This would gain 3 marks as you have used two different sources and you have linked them together to support Clare Bradley's viewpoint. You also showed the examiner that you have evaluated the source information in your final 'Therefore…' sentence.

You would then repeat this at least once.

In order to *oppose* Clare Bradley you would use the same layout, only this time you would, of course, start by saying *"I oppose the view of Clare Bradley because……."*

Here is an example in which the information in the sources that supports the view of Oliver Thomson is shown in red and the information opposing his view is shown in blue.

Victims of crime in Scotland receive satisfactory support

View of Oliver Thomson

SOURCE 1

Facts and Viewpoints

The Victims and Witnesses (Scotland) Bill was introduced by the Scottish Government and was intended to make sure that all victims and witnesses are guaranteed certain rights by law.

- The Victims and Witnesses Bill, proposes a "victim surcharge", meaning that those who commit crimes will contribute to the cost of providing support to victims eg house alarm systems and travel costs to hospital.
- Victim Support Scotland (VSS) is a voluntary group which provides a listening service for victims. Their volunteers can be easily contacted by phone, email or face to face.
- Victim Support volunteers are not trained counsellors and can only give practical information.
- Over £5 million per year is provided by the Scottish Government to support VSS and it has committed to maintaining that level of funding.
- Surveys show that victims are satisfied with the help and support given to them as victims of crime.
- The VSS run the Scottish Victim Crisis Centre (SVCC) but funding is so low that victims often get an engaged tone or an answering machine.
- The SVCC has a 9 month waiting list for victims who wish to talk about their experiences of crime.
- The Scottish Government give the SVCC £50,000 a year but staff say this is nowhere near enough to meet the demand for their services.

SOURCE 2

Scottish Crime Survey 2012

As a victim of crime, how satisfied were you with the support you received from the following?

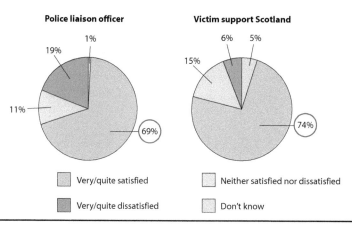

Police liaison officer

1%
19%
11%
69%

Victim support Scotland

6%   5%
15%
74%

Very/quite satisfied   Neither satisfied nor dissatisfied

Very/quite dissatisfied   Don't know

SOURCE 3

Statement by a Victim Support Campaigner

The Scottish Government has made a very positive attempt to support victims of crime in introducing the Victim and Witness Bill. They have clearly listened to what victims want and have introduced the victim surcharge which financially supports victims of crime. Victims on the whole are happy with the support they get from voluntary groups and the police. However, the funding given to some voluntary groups is simply not enough to support the level of demand for services such as counselling and advice. Some voluntary groups are not able to give full training to their staff as they can't afford it.

In your answer you **must**:

- give evidence from the sources that support Oliver Thomson's view **and**
- give evidence from the sources that oppose Oliver Thomson's view.

Your answer **must** be based on all three sources.

Now, using the layout shown above your answer could look like this:

"I can support the view of Oliver Thomson when he states 'Victims of crime in Scotland receive satisfactory support' because Source 1 states that "Surveys show that victims are satisfied with the help and support given to them as victims of crime" and this is backed up by Source 2 which shows that 74% of people in the survey were very / quite satisfied with the support they received from Victim Support Scotland and 69% were very/ quite satisfied with the support they received from a Police Liaison Officer. This is a significant majority; therefore, this shows that Oliver Thomson is correct.

You would be awarded 3 marks for this as it is a developed point, it uses and links information from two different sources and it includes evaluative language ('a significant majority'). You would then repeat this giving one more argument in support of Oliver Thomson.

Remember you MUST also oppose the view of Oliver Thomson and you can do this using exactly the same layout:

"I can oppose the view of Oliver Thomson when he states 'Victims of crime in Scotland receive satisfactory support' because Source 1 shows that although the Scottish Government give the SVCC £50,000 a year staff say this is nowhere near enough to meet the demand for their services. This is backed up by information in Source 3 which states that the funding given to some voluntary groups is simply not enough to support the level of demand for services. This shows there is significant under-funding of victim support which means the services they are able to provide are inadequate to meet victims' needs. This shows that Oliver Thomson is not correct."

Again, using words such as 'significant ' and 'inadequate' shows that you have evaluated the sources.

Making and justifying decisions

This skill involves looking at different types of information in order to come to a decision about an issue – usually this will involve making a choice between two options. Having made your decision you will have to use the sources to justify your decision.

Moira Clark is a heavy smoker who would like to give up. You must decide whether Moira should attend a smoking support group (option 1) to help her stop smoking or be given nicotine replacements (option 2).

You can choose EITHER option 1 or 2 but let's say you chose option 2. You now need to link the information about Moira to information in the option 2 box to show why that is a good option for Moira.

Factfile on Moira Clark
- Moira says she can't trust herself to give up smoking and thinks having someone check up on her is a good idea.
- *Moira has found it hard to get through the first day when she has tried to give up in the past.*
- Moira thinks it would be helpful to have others in the same situation to talk to about the experience of giving up.
- *Moira has tried to stop smoking several times before but was unsuccessful.*
- Moira says the main reason she smokes is to try and deal with the stress of her busy job.
- *Moira says the worst thing about trying to give up smoking is the cravings.*

Link 1

Link 2

Link 3

Option 1: Moira should attend a smoking support group.	Option 2: Moira should be given nicotine replacements.
• The smoking support group meets every week and the members talk about their problems and encourage each another to quit. • A nurse gives members a breath test to check if they have been smoking. • The group teaches members how to deal with stress and anxiety in different ways.	• *Nicotine replacements help to reduce the cravings that many smokers feel when they try to stop.* • *Studies show that nicotine replacements are especially effective in the first 24 hours.* • *Patients who use nicotine replacements are four times more lkely to successfully stop smoking.*

As you can see from the 'link' boxes, there is information about Moira that matches up with information in the option 2 box. Here is how you would set out your answer:

The option that would best suit Moira is option 2, nicotine replacements. The first reason for choosing option 2 is that Moira says the worst thing about trying to give up smoking is the cravings and option 2 says 'Nicotine replacements help to reduce the cravings that many smokers feel when they try to stop.' The second reason is that Moira has found it hard to get through the first day when she has tried to give up in the past and option 2 says 'Studies show that nicotine replacements are especially effective in the first 24 hours.'

At National 5 level, the question will be a bit more challenging than this. You will be expected to make a decision based on a range of sources, including written sources, graphs/diagrams and tables of statistics. These sources will be mostly straightforward but some parts may be more complex. You will also be expected to explain why you did not select the other option.

In this particular example, information that can be used to support option 1 is shaded red and option 2 is shaded blue.

> You are a government adviser. You have been asked to recommend **whether** or **not** Country Y should increase their minimum wage.

Option 1	Option 2
Increase minimum wage	Do not increase minimum wage

SOURCE 1

Country Y Factfile

Country Y is a country in Eastern Africa, with almost half the land used for farming. The average monthly wage in the country is twelve thousand shillings ($120), with the average hourly minimum wage currently100 shillings ($1). However the average monthly wage for a farm worker is six thousand shillings ($60). The government of Country Y is currently considering increasing the hourly minimum wage by a further 10%.

- The population of Country Y is 43 million, with ethnic diversity providing a vibrant culture.
- Country Y has an unemployment rate of 40%. Many argue that this is a direct result of previous increases in the hourly minimum wage.
- The agricultural sector employs a large number of workers.
- Previous increases in minimum hourly wages have been viewed negatively by businesses as well as agricultural workers.
- 43% of the population of Country Y live below the poverty line, with more than 3 million people requiring food aid.
- Tourism played a significant role in bringing money into the country; however the country suffered a series of terrorist attacks during recent years which caused a huge decline in the number of foreign visitors.
- The risk of infectious disease in the country is high with 10% of the population living with HIV/AIDS.
- Television is the main news source in cities and towns. The spread of viewing in rural areas has been slower, hampered by limited access to mains electricity.
- The President of the country stated that an increase in pay should not simply be related to the cost of living but should be linked to the productivity of the workforce.
- Housing costs in Country Y are extremely high in relation to wages — on average, rents are seven thousand shillings ($70) per month and houses are often not equipped with proper sanitation facilities, which can lead to an increased risk of poor health.

Survey of working age population

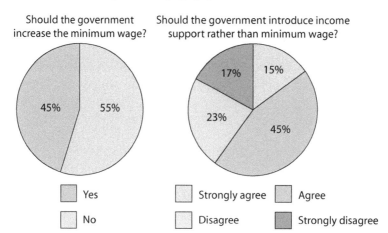

Should the government increase the minimum wage?

45% No
55% Yes

Should the government introduce income support rather than minimum wage?

15%
17%
23%
45%

☐ Yes   ☐ Strongly agree   ☐ Agree
☐ No   ☐ Disagree   ☐ Strongly disagree

Should the government introduce income support rather than increase minimum wage?

SOURCE 2

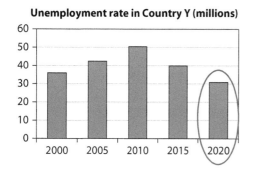

Unemployment rate in Country Y (millions)

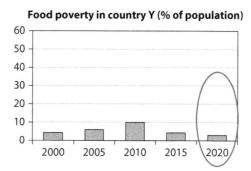

Food poverty in country Y (% of population)

SOURCE 3 Viewpoints

Viewpoints

Our members have campaigned tirelessly for an increase of 20% on the hourly minimum wage as we feel 10% is not enough. Members continually highlight how many workers have little money left after paying housing costs for the month. This affects how much money families have to spend on food and education for their children. Current low wages also restrict accessing medical treatment when required as it is simply unaffordable. Many families report that they cannot afford to pay for vaccinations for their children or access the correct medication to treat illnesses such as HIV and AIDS. It is vital that the government acts quickly.

Local Trade Union Member

The government, 3 years ago, increased the minimum hourly wage by 14%. This had a major impact on businesses as well as agricultural workers. We often suffer droughts, as well as flooding during the rainy season, and with little produce to sell we can barely afford to survive ourselves never mind pay our workers more money. A further increase in the minimum wage will result in greater unemployment, which will be a bigger issue for the government to deal with. The government must hold discussions with employers as well as the trade unions to negotiate a deal that will benefit everyone.

Local Farmer

If you choose Option 1, to recommend an increase in the minimum wage your answer will look like this:

"As a government adviser to country Y I have decided to recommend Option 1 that the country should increase the minimum wage. The first reason for my recommendation is because source 1 states 43% of the population of country Y live below the poverty line. This is supported in source 2 which shows that 55% of people surveyed said the government should increase the minimum wage. This shows that there are large numbers of people living in poverty and more than half of the people in the survey supported increasing the minimum wage".

This justification of your decision would gain 3 marks as you have:

- Clearly stated your choice at the beginning
- linked information from two different sources (Source 1 and 2)
- used information from the sources to evaluate the situation – *"This shows that there are large numbers of people living in poverty"*

As there are 10 marks available, you should try to give three justifications. In this particular question you might refer to:

- More than 3 million people requiring food aid (source 1)
- Housing costs are extremely high in relation to wages (source 1)
- Many workers have little money left after housing costs (source 3)
- Low wages restrict access to medical treatment (source 3).

Explain why you did not choose the other option.

If you do not explain why you did not choose the other option the most you can gain for this question would be 8 marks. Some students forget to do this at the end of their answer and lose marks.

Here is an example of how you would justify rejecting the other option.

" I could have chosen Option 2 as source 2 shows that both unemployment and food poverty have both been falling in recent years, however as the local trade union member in Source 3 states, 'Members continually highlight how many workers have little money left after paying housing costs for the month. This affects how much money families have to spend on food and education for their children'."

This would gain you two marks as you have clearly stated why you rejected thee other option and have used information from two different sources.

Drawing and justifying valid conclusions

In this type of question, you will be asked to look at a number of statements and come to some sort of conclusion about them by looking at the sources. At National 5, you will be given a range of sources that will be mostly straightforward but may have some more complex features.

Lower than...

Higher than...

Decreasing...

Conclusion-type words (evaluative language)

Increasing...

The same as...

Bigger...

A **conclusion** simply states what is happening or what the connection is between two things. You should use words that show 'connections'. This is called 'evaluative language'. It shows you have evaluated the information in the sources to reach a conclusion.

Here is a straightforward example:

SOURCE 1: Average wages in China

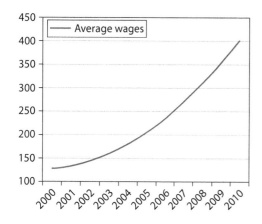

SOURCE 2: Car sales in China

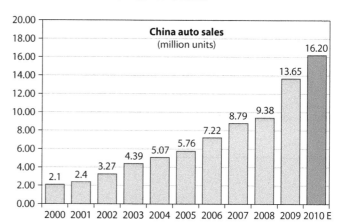

In both sources the **trend** is **increasing** and both are increasing **significantly**.

Question: What conclusion can be reached about care sales in China and average wages in China?

Look at trends in both sources – they are both increasing quite significantly, so the conclusion you can come to is:

In China, as average wages increase so does the numbers of cars sold. For example, source 1 shows that average wage increases from approximately 130 US dollars to approximately 400 US dollars and the sales of cars rises from 2.1 million cars to 16.2 million over a similar period of time.

It is important in this sort of question – as in **all** skills questions, that you use only the information in the sources. You have 'spotted' the connection and come to a conclusion.

Study Sources 1,2 and 3 and then answer the question which follows.

SOURCE 1

Poverty Factfile (2013–2014)

There are still 3–6 millsion children living in poverty in the United Kingdom. This means that a quarter (25%) of children int he UK currently live in poverty.

According to the UK Government, an average family needs to have £349 each week to meet their basic needs. The reality of living in poverty means that many families have only about £12 per day, per person to cover the basic cost of living. Children living in poverty often go without he items many children take for granted such as a bike or going on a school trip.

Poverty also has a negative impact on the health of a child with poor children experience more ill health than richer children. In addition, 24% of the poorest families cannot afford to keep their house warm compared to just 3% of wealthy families.

The UK government is trying to reduce the problem of poverty It recently set the ambitious targets that no more than 4% of children will be living in absolute poverty is when someone cannot afford the basic necessities of life, e.g. food, shelter. Relative poverty is in comparison to average incomes within a country.

Living in poverty can reduce a child's expectation of their own life and can often lead to a lifetime of poverty. Many people believe that it is the government's responsibility to help children improve their life chances and escape the cycle of poverty.

SOURCE 2

	Children Living in the Poorest Families	Children Living in the Richest Families
Average life expectancy at birth (years)	71	82
Childhood obesity rates	25%	18%
Average weekly family spending on food	£49	£70
Families who cannot afford a week's holiday per year	62%	6%

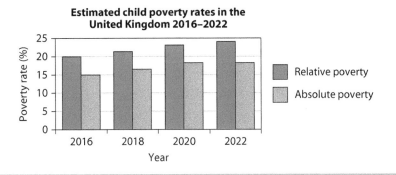

Estimated child poverty rates in the United Kingdom 2016–2022

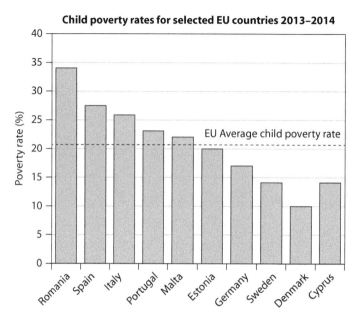

SOURCE 3

Child poverty rates for selected EU countries 2013–2014

Here is a more challenging example, more like the kind of question you are likely to face in the National 5 exam.

> Using Sources 1, 2 and 3, what **conclusions** can be drawn about the issue of child poverty?
>
> You should reach a conclusion about **each** of the following.
>
> - The impact of poverty on a child's life
> - The UK Government's progress towards meeting its targets for 2020
> - UK child poverty rates compared to other countries
>
> Your conclusions **must** be supported by evidence from the sources. You should link information within and between the sources in support of your conclusions. Your answer **must** be based on all three sources.

When you are setting out your answer, each point should have three parts:

1. Clearly state what the conclusion or relationship is and try to include some of the 'conclusion type' or 'evaluative' words outlined above

2. Say which sources show this conclusion.

3. Use evidence from the sources to 'prove' the conclusion.

For example, drawing a conclusion about 'The impact of poverty on a child's life' might look like this:

*Poverty can have a **big impact** on **many areas** of a child's life. This is backed up by information from **Source 1** which shows that children living in poverty find themselves socially excluded from everyday life and **Source 2** shows that sixty two percent of poor families cannot afford a week's holiday compared to only 6% of wealthy families.*

This conclusion would gain 3 marks:

- the conclusion is clearly stated at the beginning ('Poverty van have a big impact on many areas of a child's life')
- uses evaluative language ('big impact', 'many areas')
- Uses information from two sources (Source 1 & Source 2) to justify the conclusion

You should always aim to include these 3 parts in each conclusion although you can still gain marks by including simpler conclusions. For example "Poverty can have a big impact on many areas of a child's life" would still gain one mark.

You would then repeat this process for each of the bullet points in the question that you are to draw conclusions about.

Carrying out the assignment

As part of your National 5 course you will complete an assignment. The assignment gives you the chance to investigate any part of the course. You will choose the topic or issue, usually with a little guidance from your teacher, but the responsibility will be yours for finally deciding on the topic or issue and carrying out the investigation.

You will be expected to show that you can work independently in order to be able to:

- research and use information that is relevant
- apply your Modern Studies skills to the evidence – analyse it for bias, exaggeration, selectivity in the use of facts etc.
- use at least two methods of collecting information
- be able to say what the strengths and weaknesses of your methods were
- use the information in a way that shows that you clearly understand the topic or issue
- come to a clear conclusion about your topic or issue, supported by the evidence
- write up the results of your research under controlled conditions

Planning

The assignment is like an investigation. Before you start investigating you need to have a very clear plan.

1. **Choose your topic or issue.** Choose something you enjoyed during the course. It is much easier to investigate something you are interested in. Discuss this with your teacher. It could also be something that you are interested in that has relevance to Modern Studies but is not covered in your course. Possible topics include:
   - Pressure group methods
   - The power of the media
   - The growing power of China and/or India
   - Inequality (this could focus on women or ethnic minorities or another group)
   - Scotland's health

2. **The hypothesis.** Once you have decided on your topic or issue, it is a good idea to have a 'starting statement' that you then must try to prove or disprove. This is called a **hypothesis**. For example:
   - Pressure groups are more effective if they break the law.
   - The media in Scotland does not have any influence on how people behave.
   - China is more important in the world today than the USA.
   - Scotland needs India more than India needs Scotland.

- Women have achieved equality in Scotland today.
- Scotland is no longer the 'sick man of Europe'.

As you can see, these statements are worded in such a way that you will have to look at both sides before you can 'prove' or 'disprove' them.

3. **What you aim to find out.** In order to prove or disprove your hypothesis, you must find out evidence for it and against it. This is easier if you 'break it down' into separate **aims**, which are what you want to find out anyway. For example, if your hypothesis was 'Women have achieved equality in the UK today', your aims could be:

- **Aim 1** – I aim to find out if women are equally represented in the Scottish and UK Parliaments.
- **Aim 2** – I aim to find out how female earnings compare with male earnings in Scotland.

4. **Methods.** For each aim, think what might be the best ways to find out the information you need. As you will see below, there are many different ways of finding out information and you must decide which is most suitable. For example, for aim 1 (I aim to find out if women are equally represented in the Scottish and UK Parliaments):

- use the websites of the Scottish and UK Parliaments to find out the numbers of women in the Scottish Parliament and the UK Parliament
- write a structured letter to your local MSP and MP to find out what roles women play in the Scottish and UK Parliaments

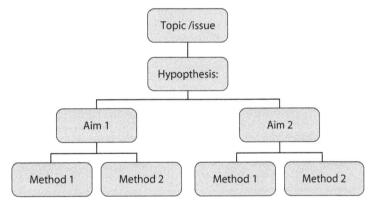

You do NOT have to use two different methods for each Aim but you MUST use at least TWO different methods during your research as you will be asked to say what their strengths and weaknesses were when you used them.

Primary and secondary information

There are two main types of information that all researchers use – primary information and secondary information.

- Primary information – information that you yourself have collected straight from the source. Primary information can come from:
    - writing letters for information
    - interviews (face-to-face, by telephone, by video conference)

- surveys and questionnaires
- statistics
- taking notes on a visit
- Secondary information – information that you can use but which someone else will have produced, for example:
  - websites: detail different online resources, e.g. websites, online news sites like BBC, Youtube, social media. Using 2 different online sources is acceptable
  - texts
  - the media (TV, radio and newspapers)
  - reports

In the assignment you should use both primary and secondary information. In the Assignment you can use both primary and secondary information, although this is not necessary to gain full marks so long as two different methods are used.

Research methods – strengths and weaknesses

As part of the assignment you will also have to evaluate your methods – in other words, say what each method's strengths and weaknesses were. Use this table to help you. BEWARE these are generic points about each method. When evaluating your method, you have to talk about the specific strengths and weaknesses of YOUR sources i.e. One strength of my survey was …

Research method	Strengths	Weaknesses
Writing letters for information	• You can ask specific questions about your assignment. • You are asking someone who can give you an 'expert' opinion. • It does not cost much.	• Many letters get no reply. • It is sometimes difficult to know who to send it to. • You can't ask follow-up questions.
Carrying out an interview	• You can ask specific questions about your assignment. • You are asking someone who can give you an 'expert' opinion. • It does not cost much. • You can also ask follow-up questions.	• Not everyone is happy to be interviewed. • They may not tell you all of the facts. • They may be biased.
Internet searches	• Many places and people now have Internet access. • There is a lot of information available on the web. • Some sources are very reliable.	• You need Internet access. • There may be far too much information. • Some information is biased or exaggerated.

Using a library	• Most librarians will help you find information. • They may keep back copies of newspapers etc. • Most libraries have Internet access.	• Information in books can be too 'old' for Modern Studies. • Some reference books cannot be borrowed. • They are not always open when you need them.
Carrying out surveys and questionnaires	• Good for finding out people's opinions on an issue. • If you ask enough people you will get a good idea of general public opinion. • You can show results graphically.	• Poorly worded questions get poor answers. • If sent by post you may not get a reply. • Online surveys can be answered many times by the same person.
Taking structured notes on a visit	• You may be able to speak to someone during the visit. • Notes can be referred to later. • You may be able to take pictures to include in your assignment.	• They can take a long time to organise especially if special permission is needed. • You may not have much time. • You may not be allowed to take pictures.
Using the media	• Information is up-to-date. • There are many sources you can trust, e.g. news from the BBC, Sky, Channel 4 etc. • It is easy to access many different types of media.	• Print media can be biased. • You may only get the main points on broadcast media. • There might be too much information available from all the different types of media.
Video conferencing using applications such as Skype, FaceTime etc	• You can ask specific questions about your assignment. • You are asking someone who can give you an 'expert' opinion. • It does not cost much. • You can also ask follow-up questions. • You can speak to people in other parts of the country or the world.	• Same disadvantages as interviews. • You need the correct equipment, which can be expensive.

How useful are sources – using the 'three Rs'

An important part of investigating is deciding how useful a particular source is, especially as we are now able to access so much information using the Internet. Here are three key questions you should ask yourself:

Recent   Reliable

The three Rs

Relevant

1. How **recent** is the source? In Modern Studies, information can go out of date quite quickly. Many organisations and governments will bring out annual (yearly) reports. Try to use the most up-to-date ones.

2. Is this source **relevant**? Will it help me with one (or more) of my aims?

3. Is it **reliable**? Can you 'trust' this source? In order to decide on this you need to know:
   - Who made it? Was it the Government? A trusted media company?
   - Why did they make it? Some sources might have been produced to make a particular point or support a particular point of view.

There is an example on page 23. Imagine you have chosen the hypothesis: "Scotland is no longer the 'sick man of Europe'" and one of your aims is to find out the effect of soft drinks on obesity in children. Using the three Rs will help you to decide if this is a useful source for your assignment.

Writing up

- The assignment makes up 20% of the marks for the course.
- The assignment will be marked out of 20.
- 10 marks for evaluating your two research methods (i.e. their strengths and weaknesses)
- 6 marks for analysing and explaining the key points of your investigation using your research and your own knowledge
- 4 marks for reaching a well-supported conclusion, supported by evidence, about the topic or issue. Have you proven or disproven your Hypothesis?
- You will write-up your assignment under strict conditions.
- You will have 1 hour to do this.
- You will be given a guide or 'template' to follow when you are doing the write-up.
- You will be allowed to take two A4 Research Evidence Sheets in to the write up with you, consisting of material you collected during your research.
- You MUST refer to these sheets in the write up but you must not simply copy information from them. You are encouraged not to put too much info into your RES.

An example of The Three Rs

Let's say your Hypothesis was "Childhood obesity is not a problem in Scotland". Here is an example of a recent reliable and relevant source. This could in fact be included in your Research Sheets.

The ⚔ Herald

Reliable? The Herald is 'quality' newspaper and is a trusted source although

Published on 15th May 2018

Recent? When this book was written this was very recent. Avoid sources that are out of date.

Nicola Sturgeon has set the goal of reducing childhood obesity by 50% in the next 12 years – with TV chef Jamie Oliver saying the target shows Scotland's First Minister "cares" about youngsters' health. The Scottish Government will formally include the ambition in its Healthy Weight and Diet plan, which is due to be published this summer. Ms Sturgeon announced the move as she met the celebrity chef, who has previously campaigned to make school dinners healthier, to discuss the problems of childhood obesity and healthy eating. Almost a third (29%) of Scottish children are at risk of being overweight, with 14% at risk of obesity, according to the latest figures.

Relevant? The article contains information that will help you with your Aim.

Reliable? BBC is a trusted source and they quote from trusted organisations

Nicola Sturgeon and Jamie Oliver

The UK political system

The branches of government

EXAM TIP

The UK, India and the USA are all representative democracies and they all separate the powers of government, giving each branch responsibility for a different power. However, in the UK we do not have a separately elected 'President'.

The Government of the UK, like many democracies, divides the powers of government among different 'branches' so that no one branch has too much power. This is known as the **separation of powers**.

- Legislative power – The House of Commons and the House of Lords have the power to make new laws or change existing ones.
- Executive power – The Prime Minister and the Cabinet make decisions for the day-to-day running of the country.
- Judicial power – The Supreme Court and the courts system make sure the laws are upheld and enforced.

The UK Parliament

The UK Parliament is bi-cameral, which means that it is made up of two 'chambers' or houses: the House of Commons and the House of Lords.

The House of Commons is the elected chamber, and the key features are as follows:

- There are 650 MPs.
- Each MP represents a single constituency.
- The MPs are elected using a First Past the Post voting system.
- It is responsible for the legislative function of government.
- It scrutinises the government of the day.

The House of Lords is not elected. It is made up of two categories of lords:

- Lords 'spiritual' are members because of the posts they hold in the Church of England.
- Lords 'temporal' are either 'life' peers (another name for lords) whose title dies with them, or they are 'hereditary' peers who have inherited their titles.

The House of Lords can introduce new bills and can review and change bills sent to it from the Commons, although the House of Commons has the 'final say'.

The UK Government

The executive function of government is carried out in the UK by the Prime Minister and the Cabinet. After a general election, the political party that has the most MPs (a majority) usually forms the government.

The Judiciary (the courts system)

In the UK, the courts are responsible for making sure that the laws are enforced and for punishing lawbreakers. There is not a single system for the whole of the UK, as the courts systems are different in England, Northern Ireland, Scotland and Wales, but in each case there will be different levels of courts from the local level to the national level.

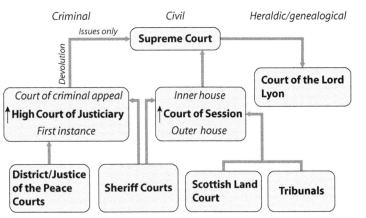

Constitutional monarchy

The UK is often described as a 'constitutional monarchy'. This means that the monarch (currently Queen Elizabeth II) is the head of state and the government of the country is carried out 'on behalf' of the monarch by the various parts of the devolved Government of the UK. But how important is the monarch?

Queen Elizabeth II

- The role is now largely 'ceremonial'.
- 'Royal prerogatives' such as awarding honours or signing treaties are decided by the government.
- The monarch can act as a focus of national unity, such as during wars.
- The monarch represents the UK on ceremonial occasions and state visits.

The devolved governments of the UK

In the UK we have a devolved system of government, meaning that certain powers have been transferred from the UK Parliament to other decision-making bodies in Northern Ireland, Scotland and Wales. These transferred powers are called **devolved powers**, and those that are kept by the UK Parliament are called **reserved powers**. The work of the Scottish Parliament and Government will be dealt with in more detail later.

Quick Test

1. Explain how separation of the powers works in the UK.
2. Describe how the two chambers of the UK Parliament are made up.
3. What evidence is there that the monarch has no real power today?
4. What is meant by devolution?

Participating in a representative democracy

What is a representative democracy?

In a democracy the people have the right to participate in the decision-making for the country. In modern democracies such as the UK, this is done by choosing representatives who then take decisions on behalf of the electorate. Because of this process of electing representatives, the UK is described as a 'representative democracy'.

Features of a democracy

Throughout this book, there will be descriptions of other political systems in India, China and the USA and, in the case of China and India particularly, we will ask, 'how democratic are they?' In order to answer this question it is necessary to know that the main features of a democracy are:

- Guaranteed rights, such as the right to vote and freedom of speech.
- Regular, fair and free elections.
- A free media not controlled by the government.
- A genuine choice between political parties.

Representative democracy

1. The people...
2. Choose/elect...
3. Representatives
4. Who make...
5. Decisions and laws...
6. Which apply to...

How democratic is the UK?

Guaranteed rights – The Human Rights Act

The Human Rights Act introduced in 2000 guarantees that public bodies such as the courts, police, councils and state schools, must not take away or damage the rights laid down in the European Charter of Human Rights, which include: i) The right to life; ii) The right to a fair trial; iii) No punishment without the law; iv) Freedom of thought, belief and religion.

Other laws, such as the Equality Act 2010, make sure that people are not discriminated against because of things like gender, disability or ethnic group.

Regular, fair and free elections

In the UK, citizens can vote for representatives at different levels. These elections are regular, free and fair.

A free media not controlled by the government

In the UK we have a very wide choice of media, from print, to radio/TV and social media. For the most part, the media are free to report on events in the country and the wider world without government interference.

UK citizens can vote for these bodies

- The European Parliament
- Local Authorities (councils)
- The UK Parliament
- The Scottish Parliament (or the Welsh and Northern Ireland Assemblies)

A genuine choice of political parties

In the UK there are many political parties to choose from.

UK Parliament election 2017

- Conservative Party
- Labour Party
- Liberal Democratic Party
- Democratic Unionist Party
- Scottish National Party
- Plaid Cymru
- Green Party
- Sinn Fein (do not attend)

Scottish Parliament election 2016

- Scottish National Party
- Labour Party
- Conservative Party
- Liberal Democratic Party
- Green Party

EXAM TIP

According to Reporters Without Borders, which ranks countries according to how free their media is, the UK was ranked 40/180. The organisation stated that the UK was 'one of the worst-ranked Western European countries in the World Press Freedom Index' partly due to the Investigatory Powers Act, which they described as 'the most extreme surveillance legislation in UK history'.

How can citizens participate in a democracy?

This can involve more than voting. People are participating whenever they try to influence things around them, e.g. in their workplace, in the local community, in the nation as a whole or even in European and international affairs.

Voting: Choosing between different candidates, usually from different political parties, to represent an area or group of people.

Joining and being active in organisations: Becoming a member of an organisation such as a trade union, a political party or a pressure group.

Taking direct action: Action taken to directly influence decisions on a particular issue. Includes activities such as protests, demonstrations, picketing, petitioning, striking or organising campaigns.

Lobbying elected representatives: Trying to influence the decisions of elected representatives by 'lobbying' them. Individuals or groups of people arrange meetings with their representatives to try to persuade them to do something or, indeed, stop doing something.

Using the media: This might include using social media such as Facebook and Twitter or getting publicity in newspapers and on television.

Quick Test

1. Describe how a representative democracy works.
2. What are the main features of a democracy?
3. What evidence is there that Scotland and the UK are democratic?
4. Which two methods of participating do you think are most effective? Give reasons for your choices.

The Government of Scotland

Devolved and reserved powers

As a result of devolution, Scotland once again has its own parliament. The Scottish Parliament has responsibility for certain **devolved** powers, while the UK Parliament remains responsible for certain **reserved** powers. Some of these are listed below.

Devolved powers	Reserved powers
Health	Foreign Affairs
Education	Defence
Housing	International Relations
Social Work	Economic Policy
Environment	Immigration and Nationality
Police and Fire	Social Security
Agriculture, Forestry and Fishing	Energy: electricity, coal, gas and nuclear power

> **EXAM TIP**
>
> The 2012 Scotland Act devolved more powers to the Scottish Parliament, including: increased borrowing powers, more control over taxation, and power over air guns, drink-driving and speeding limits.

The Government of Scotland

Following the Scottish Parliamentary Elections of 2016, the SNP won more seats than any other party. Although they did not win an overall majority of the seats, as the biggest single party they formed the Scottish Government. The Scottish Government is the executive branch of government made up of the First Minister and the Cabinet. It is responsible for all devolved powers.

The First Minister

The First Minster is the leader of the largest party and is the head of the Scottish Government. At the time this book was written, the Scottish Government was led by Nicola Sturgeon. The First Minister chooses the members of the Cabinet and has the overall responsibility for deciding on the policies of the Scottish Government. She also represents Scotland in dealings with the UK and other countries.

The Cabinet

The Cabinet has 25 members including the First Minister, Cabinet Secretaries and Ministers. Each member of the Cabinet has responsibility for a certain part of the work of the government. The Cabinet coordinates the work of the various parts of government as well as putting forward the large majority of new bills.

The Cabinet of the Scottish Government

The Scottish Parliament

The modern Scottish Parliament opened in May 1999. Unlike the UK Parliament, it is a unicameral parliament (i.e. a single chamber). It is made up of 129 MSPs and 73 of those MSPs represent individual constituencies. They are elected using a **first past the post** system. The other 56 MSPs represent eight 'regions' (seven MSPs per region). They are elected using a system called the **additional member system.**

What powers does the Scottish Parliament have?

- It is responsible for the legislative function, i.e. all new laws must be passed by the parliament. It can change, pass or reject bills.
- It can hold the Scottish Government to account through:
  - asking questions at Question Time
  - committees that look closely at the work of the government
  - debates in the chamber of the Parliament.
- It represents the views of the Scottish people.
- It discusses issues affecting the lives of the people of Scotland.
- Since 2016 with the introduction of the Scottish Rate of Income Tax, the Scottish Government has the power to raise or lower income tax across a range of incomes for people living in Scotland.

The key principles of the Scottish Parliament

The work of the Scottish Parliament is based on certain key principles. This is how they are described on the Scottish Parliament website:

- **Accountable** – the Scottish Parliament is answerable to the people of Scotland. The Scottish Parliament should hold the Scottish Government to account.

- **Open and Encourages Participation** – the Scottish Parliament should be accessible and involve the people of Scotland in its decisions as much as possible.
- **Power Sharing** – power should be shared among the Scottish Government, the Scottish Parliament and the people of Scotland.
- **Equal Opportunities** – the Scottish Parliament should treat all people fairly.

The debating chamber at the Scottish Parliament

Quick Test

1. Briefly, describe the role of the First Minister and the Cabinet in Scotland.
2. In what ways can the Scottish Parliament hold the Scottish Government to account?
3. What other powers does the Scottish Parliament have?
4. Which of the four principles of the Scottish Parliament do you think is most important in a democracy? Give reasons for your answer.

Scotland's voting system

Elections for the Scottish Parliament

Why is it important for people in a democracy to use their vote?

- It is one of the most effective ways for people to show how they feel about how well (or not!) they think the government has been running the country.
- Elections in a democracy allow the peaceful changeover from one government to another. In some non-democratic countries governments have only been changed after violent struggle.
- If governments did not have to regularly 'answer' to the people, they might not act in the best interests of the people.
- People who do not vote may not have a moral right to criticise the government.

The Scottish voting system

Scotland uses a proportional representation (PR) voting system. PR systems try to get a closer match between the proportion of votes a party wins and its proportion of seats in parliament. The Scottish system is a 'hybrid' system, i.e. a combination of two voting systems – First Past the Post and the Additional Member System. Voters in Scotland have two votes: for constituency MSPs and for regional MSPs.

First Past the Post for constituency MSPs	Additional Member System for regional MSPs
Scotland is divided up into 73 constituencies (also called 'seats' because the winners get to take a seat in the Scottish Parliament).	Scotland is divided up into eight much larger areas called 'regions'.
In each constituency, you vote for the candidate you want to win.	Seven MSPs are elected per region. You vote for the party you want, such as the SNP, Labour, etc.
The candidate who has the most votes becomes the MSP for that constituency.	Before the election the parties compile a list of names for each region, in order of preference.
This voting system is called **First Past the Post**: the first past the winning post wins the race.	Once it is clear how many seats a party has won, then that number of candidates from their list become MSPs.
In total there are 129 MSPs: 73 constituency MSPs and 56 regional MSPs.	

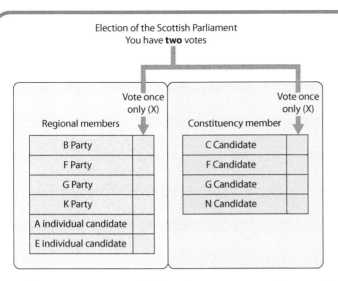

Election of the Scottish Parliament
You have **two** votes

Regional members	Vote once only (X)
B Party	
F Party	
G Party	
K Party	
A individual candidate	
E individual candidate	

Constituency member	Vote once only (X)
C Candidate	
F Candidate	
G Candidate	
N Candidate	

EXAM TIP

Always make sure you know the results of the most recent election so that you can refer to them in your answer. The examiner is looking for up-to-date knowledge.

Advantages and disadvantages of Scotland's voting system

	Advantages	Disadvantages
First Past the Post	<ul><li>Keeps a strong link between the MSPs and a specific constituency.</li><li>It is easy to understand and produces a quick result.</li><li>It usually (not always) produces a single party government that doesn't rely on other parties to get its policies through parliament.</li><li>It often produces a strong opposition party that constantly keeps the government 'on its toes'.</li></ul>	<ul><li>A constituency can be won with much fewer than half the votes. The winner only needs to have one more vote than their nearest rival.</li><li>Benefits parties who have a lot of support concentrated in certain areas but not parties with support more spread out.</li><li>Some people may not bother voting if the candidate or party they support in their constituency does not have a chance of coming first.</li></ul>
Additional Member System	<ul><li>Reduces the 'disproportionality' of votes to seats that FPTP often creates. For example, the Conservative Party won only three constituency seats in the 2011 Scottish election but they won 12 seats from the AMS vote.</li><li>Produced two stable and cooperative coalition governments in the first two elections. Can create a government that has a broader range of views in it.</li><li>Parties can use their regional list MSPs to make up shortfalls in, for example, female or ethnic minority MSP numbers by putting them at the top of their lists.</li></ul>	<ul><li>List candidates are chosen by the parties. Voters do not vote for individual candidates, so the constituents might not know much about their list MSP.</li><li>List MSPs do not have a constituency to represent. This has caused disagreements in the Scottish Parliament between list and constituency MSPs about who should be doing what.</li><li>One of the coalition partners may be quite small but will have a lot of influence as part of the government.</li></ul>

Quick Test

1.   Give three reasons why it is important for voters in a democracy to use their vote.

2.   Why is the first past the post system seen by some as 'unfair'?

3.   What are the advantages and disadvantages of coalition governments?

Scottish independence

The referendum

On 18 September 2014, people in Scotland took part in a referendum in which they were asked the question 'Should Scotland be an independent country?'. The result of the referendum was that 55.3% voted 'No' and 44.7% voted 'Yes'. At the time it was thought that the question of independence had been settled 'for a generation'. However, in another referendum across the whole of the UK in 2016 in which the people were asked if they wanted to leave or remain in the EU, 51.89% voted 'Leave' and 48.11% voted 'Remain'. In Scotland, however, the vote was 62% Remain and 38% Leave. Supporters of independence in Scotland, including the SNP, argued that this meant that there should be another vote on independence (Indyref 2) at some point in the future.

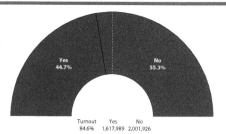

Yes 44.7%   No 55.3%

Turnout 84.6%   Yes 1,617,989   No 2,001,926

Result of Scottish Independence Referendum

Different viewpoints

Those who support independence believe that Scotland would be better off as a separate independent country, while those who are against independence believe that Scotland is better off as part of the UK. There are also those who believe that Scotland should have more powers within the UK and that the Scottish Parliament should have even more power over things like raising and spending taxation and legal powers.

Frequently asked questions

1. Q. Would Scotland keep the monarchy?
   A. Yes and it would also remain within the Commonwealth.
2. Q. Would an independent Scotland keep the pound?
   A. Yes, for the moment. In May 2018 the SNP published its Growth Commission Report, which said that Scotland would keep the pound for possibly up to ten years. It might produce a new Scottish currency, but only if certain 'strict conditions' are met.

Issues: if Scotland did keep sterling would it mean the Bank of England would still decide on things like interest rates in Scotland? When will the 'time be right' for Scotland to introduce its own currency?

3. Q. How would North Sea oil be affected?
   A. The SNP believes Scotland is entitled to 'keep' over 80% of the income from North Sea oil. This is called the 'geographic' share.

North Sea oil was worth £14.3 billion in 2015–16

Issue: the UK government does not agree that this will be the case. If the 'split' was according to the size of the population of Scotland and the UK, this would bring Scotland's share down to 9%.

4. Q. Would Scotland have its own armed forces?

   A. Yes. The SNP state that The Scottish Defence Force would consist of one naval base, one air base and one mobile army brigade.

Issues: Would Scotland need to buy more naval ships, such as submarines, to have an adequate size navy or would it 'share' with the rest of the UK? Would people serving in the UK armed forces be allowed to choose whether to stay in the UK or join the Scottish Defence Force?

5. Q. Would the UK's nuclear submarines have to leave their current base at Faslane on the Clyde?

   A. Yes. The SNP is against nuclear weapons and has stated that an independent Scotland would not allow nuclear missiles in Scotland.

Issues: who will pay for the cost of removal? How long will it take?

6. Q. Would Scotland stay in the European Union?

   A. Yes. The SNP state that since 2004, ten new countries joined the EU – 'six of them smaller than Scotland, and six of which have become independent since 1990.' They see no difficulty with Scotland joining.

Issues: some argue that this would not be automatic and that Scotland would have to re-apply for membership of the EU. There are no examples where a 'part' of an existing EU member has applied to join following independence. When this book was written, the UK was in the process of leaving the EU (Brexit), so Scotland may no longer be 'part' of an existing EU member.

7. Q. Will Scotland stay in NATO?

   A. Yes. The SNP at its 2012 conference voted to stay in NATO but as a 'non-nuclear' member.

Issues: The SNP is a non-nuclear party but NATO has nuclear weapons. Also, Scotland would have to apply to join as a separate country and some NATO members such as Spain might block membership. Spain is concerned that Scottish independence might 'set an example' for parts of Spain that also want independence.

8. Q. Would there be 'border controls' at the Scotland–England border?

   A. No. Although there will be a 'Scottish passport', the SNP has stated there will be 'no checks or delays' when crossing into England, and there would be 'no customs posts or demand for passports'.

Issues: If an independent Scotland joined the EU and the rest of the UK has left (Brexit), there could possibly be checks of some kind on people and goods going between an EU member (Scotland) and a non-EU member (the rest of the UK).

Quick Test

1. Describe the three different viewpoints about Scotland's position in the UK.

2. Decide which are the three strongest arguments for and against Scottish independence and summarise them in your own words.

3. Which do you think are the three biggest 'issues'? Again, summarise them in your own words.

Election campaigns

Campaign methods

In the run up to an election, political parties will put a lot of time, effort and money (if they can afford it!) into the election campaign. The main purpose of an election campaign is to persuade as many voters as possible to vote for the party.

At the national level, the parties campaign using a number of methods, including party election broadcasts. These are short TV programmes that often use advertising techniques such as slogans to win voters. Leading politicians from the main parties may also appear on political talk shows, such as 'Newsnight Scotland', and will tour the country visiting as many constituencies as possible, especially 'marginal' constituencies where they have a chance of gaining a seat.

Other campaign methods include:

- putting up campaign posters and billboards
- posting leaflets through letterboxes
- canvassing, i.e. going round the doors asking people to vote for the party
- using touring loudspeaker vans
- using social media such as Twitter and Facebook to contact voters
- organising transport to the polling station for elderly or disabled voters
- holding a 'hustings' – a public meeting where the main candidates will debate and answer questions from the public

EXAM TIP

If an exam question asks you how members of a political party can help during an election campaign, you should describe the above activities but you can also add fundraising for the party and, of course, voting for the party at the election.

The candidates

People who put themselves forward for election will need to have certain qualities and skills in order to become an effective representative. There is little point, for example, in someone who is very 'shy' putting themselves forward!

Hard-working

Believes in the party's policies

Confident

Trustworthy

Gets on well with people

Good communicator – able to speak and write well

Role of the mass media in election campaigns

One of the main features of an election campaign is its coverage in the mass media: television, radio and newspapers and online media. The media is the main way the electorate get information about politics.

- **The broadcast media** – All broadcast media in the UK (i.e. all radio and TV channels), must by law remain neutral in politics. It is important that the broadcast media does not 'take sides' as this is the way most people get their information about politics. Broadcast media are expected to give 'fair' coverage to the main political parties and more time is given to the parties who had a large amount of support in previous elections.

- **The print media** – Newspapers (or the press) are privately owned. Two people, Rupert Murdoch and Lord Rothermere, between them own over half of the newspapers in the UK. Newspapers will often support a particular party and, just before an election, will often 'urge' their readers to vote for that party. They do, however, have the responsibility to keep the laws of the country with regard to such things as libel laws or the Official Secrets Act. In other words, they cannot print lies or anything that would threaten the security of the nation.

- **Social media** – It is said that the 2010 UK general election was the first 'social media' election, with most parties and many candidates using Facebook and Twitter, and by the time of the UK election in 2017 all of the main parties were using social media to get their message across. For example, the Conservative Party is said to have spent £1.2 million on online ads, while the Labour Party used targeted online ads in the areas they thought they might take seats from the other parties. Although it was believed at the time of the 2017 election that social media played a large part in the election, especially in getting young people out to vote, several studies including ones by YouGov and The British Election Survey have shown that:
  - although there was an increase in young people voting, there was also an increase in other age groups
  - of the young people who did turn out to vote, Labour increased its share
  - Jeremy Corbyn had about 2.5 times more Facebook followers than Theresa May. Even though young people do get most of their news through social media, surveys after the election showed that the news they trusted most on their social media platforms was from organisations like the BBC and newspapers such as the *Guardian* and the *Daily Mail*.
  - Even although young people do get most of their news through social media, surveys after the election showed that the news they trusted most on their social media platforms were organisation like the BBC and newspapers such as the *Guardian* and the *Daily Mail*.

Quick Test

1. What is the main difference between the way newspapers and the broadcast media report on politics?

2. Choose any three election campaign methods and say why you think they are effective.

3. Do you think newspapers should be allowed to 'back' a particular party in an election? Give reasons for your answers.

4. Describe the role of social media during election campaigns.

The work of an MSP

How do MSPs represent their constituents?

How can MSPs act on behalf of their constituents both inside the Scottish Parliament and in their constituencies and regions?

In constituencies and regions

- MSPs attend events and meetings to listen to the views of constituents and people from other groups and organisations, such as local employers.

- MSPs can contact officials, government departments, etc. to raise issues on behalf of their constituents.

- MSPs meet with or contact other elected representatives such as councillors and MPs.

Ross Greer became the youngest ever MSP when he was elected for the Green Party in 2016

- MSPs can join or support local pressure groups or campaigns to add 'weight' (importance) to a local issue, perhaps attracting media attention.

- MSPs hold regular surgeries where constituents can come along and discuss an issue or a problem they need help with.

Question Time | Debates

MSPs inside the Scottish Parliament

Members Bills | Committees

Decision Time

Inside the Scottish Parliament

There are many opportunities for MSPs to represent their constituents in the Scottish Parliament.

- **Question Time** – MSPS can ask questions at the different types of Question Time:

  - General Question Time takes place on a Thursday for 20 minutes. MSPs can put questions to any member of the Scottish Government.

  - Question Time: 40 minutes when Ministers and Cabinet Secretaries who are in charge of different government departments such as Education and Lifelong Learning answer questions about the work of their departments.

  - First Minister's Question Time takes place each Thursday for 30 minutes. The First Minister answers questions about the work and actions of the Scottish Government.

- **Debates** – MSPs can suggest topics to debate in the Parliament by putting forward a motion for discussion. They can also suggest amendments to motions put forward by other MSPs. There are different types of debates:

  - Members Business is when a motion is debated that has been put forward by an MSP who is not a Minister or a Cabinet Secretary. These debates will usually be about a current issue or event that the MSP is concerned about, or something to do with that MSP's constituency or region.

– General Debates: these are the discussions that take place about the issues of the day, the work of the Scottish Government, new suggestions for laws etc.

- **Member's Bills** – A Bill is a suggestion for a new law. Most bills are executive bills introduced by the government but MSPs can also put forward member's bills. These might be things that MSP feels strongly about. For example, MSP Keith Harding managed to get a law passed that meant dog owners could be fined for not clearing up their dog's 'mess'!

Witnesses give evidence to the Justice Committee

- **Decision Time** – At the end of each day in the Scottish Parliament, 30 minutes is set aside for MSPs to vote on all of the motions, bills, amendments to bills, etc. that have been discussed that day.

- **Committees** – MSPs are usually members of at least one committee, a small group of between five and 15 MSPs. Committees have several functions:

    – To scrutinise (keep a close eye on) the work of the Scottish Government.

    – To carry out enquiries into current issues.

    – To carefully look at new bills that might affect the things the committee has responsibility for. They will often suggest changes to the bill or they may themselves put forward a new bill.

    – Call 'witnesses' to their meetings to get their views and opinions on matters being discussed.

How constituents can contact their MSPs

> **EXAM TIP**
>
> An excellent place to get up-to-date examples to include in examination answers is the Scottish Parliament website where the 'Parliamentary Business' section lists things such as new bills being introduced and the current work of committees.

Constituents can write, email or telephone their MSP at their constituency office. They can also attend any MSP surgeries held in the constituencies. Another face-to-face method is lobbying – going to meet MSPs at the Scottish Parliament. Many MSPs also use social media, such as Twitter and Facebook.

Quick Test

1. Describe three ways in which an MSP can act on behalf of the people they represent within their constituencies or regions.

2. Apart from committees, which two methods do you think are most effective for MSPs to get their views known inside the Scottish Parliament? Give reasons for your choices.

3. What are committees and what do they do?

Political parties

A political party is made up of people with the same or similar views. Each party will put forward candidates at elections and aim to get these candidates elected so that they can influence the decisions made by elected bodies such as councils and parliaments. In Scotland and the UK, this means that political parties can take part in elections for local authorities or councils, the Scottish Parliament, the UK Parliament, or the European Parliament.

Political parties are also expected to represent the views of their members and not just those of the party leaders.

Political parties in Scotland and the UK

This table shows the political parties and how many candidates they each managed to get elected in recent elections.

Scottish Parliament election 2016	Seats won	UK Parliament election 2017	Seats won
Scottish National Party	63	Conservative Party	318
Conservative Party	31	Labour Party	262
Labour Party	24	Scottish National Party	35
Liberal Democratic Party	5	Liberal Democratic Party	12
Green Party	6	Democratic Unionist Party	10
Independent	0	Others	13

As you can see from this table, the largest parties in Scotland are the SNP, Conservatives, Labour and Liberal Democrats, and in the UK it is Conservative, Labour and SNP.

The policies of the main parties in Scotland

Policies are the ideas that political parties want to put into place. Before an election, each party will publish its manifesto to set out its policies. If a party is elected to government, they are expected to put these policies into place.

Here is a summary of the manifestos of the largest political parties before the 2016 Scottish Parliament election.

Scottish National Party	<ul><li>Increase NHS spending by £500 million by the end of the current parliament.</li><li>Introduce a new cancer plan to improve prevention, early diagnosis and treatment of cancer.</li><li>Keep free prescriptions and free personal and nursing care.</li><li>Every child in early education in the most deprived communities will have an additional teacher or childcare graduate by 2018.</li><li>Reduce the education attainment gap between poorer and better off children through the Scottish Attainment Fund.</li><li>Make sure all of Scotland has broadband, build 50,000 affordable new homes and improve transport links.</li><li>Hold another referendum on Scottish independence if public opinion supports it or if Scotland is taken out of the EU against its will.</li></ul>

Labour Party	• Guarantee an appointment at a GP surgery within 48 hours. • Ensure mental health is given the same priority as physical health. • Use the proceeds from the 'sugar tax' to invest in after-school sport. • Reduce the gap between 'the richest and the rest' in classrooms. • Increase income tax for those earning more than £150,000 to invest in education. • Tackle fuel poverty through a Warm Homes Act. • Build 60,000 affordable homes, with 45,000 of those for rent by councils, housing associations and co-operatives.
Conservative Party	• Oppose any attempt by the SNP to hold a second independence referendum. • Keep the same rates of income tax as in the rest of the UK. • Extend free nursery hours to more disadvantaged one- and two-year-olds. • University graduates pay back £1,500 for every year of their degree once they are earning more than £20,000 a year. • Making sure spending on health keeps up with inflation. • Build 100,000 new homes in the next 5 years, with half being classed as 'affordable'.
Liberal Democrat Party	• Strongly oppose another 'divisive' independence referendum. • Add a penny on income tax in Scotland to be spent on improving education and mental health. • Make sure the state pension keeps up with inflation. • Extend free childcare and encourage new fathers to take time off with an additional month's paid paternity leave. • Make sure that Scotland never has another shortage of GPs. • Build 300,000 homes a year across the UK by 2022. • Oppose national testing in schools.

EXAM TIP

Remember that this is only a small selection of each party's policies and that parties will often change or replace their policies, so it is a good idea to visit their websites to see what their most recent policies are. Remember, the examiner in Modern Studies will be looking for recent, relevant examples.

Quick Test

1. What are the main purposes of political parties?
2. Describe political party strength in Scotland and the UK following the elections of 2016 and 2017. Are there any similarities between the two elections?
3. Explain what a manifesto is.
4. Looking at the manifestos of the main parties in Scotland, which party would you support? You must give clear reasons for your choice.

Pressure groups

A pressure group is an organisation of people who share similar views or goals. Pressure groups usually want to change something, stop something or start something happening. In other words they try to influence decision-making by 'pressuring' individuals, organisations, elected representatives, parliaments, businesses and the media.

Types of pressure group

Pressure groups can vary in size from small, local groups that may only exist for a short time, such as a group set up to save a local playing field from being built over, to much larger national or international groups who campaign for a much wider 'cause', such as nuclear disarmament or the environment. The type of pressure group where the members try to 'promote' the same 'cause' (for example Greenpeace), is called a **promotional pressure group**. Pressure groups that try to protect the interests of a 'section' or group of people in society are called **sectional pressure groups**. Examples of these would include trade unions such as UNISON.

Unison members outside Glasgow City Chambers demanding equal pay for women

The rights and responsibilities of pressure groups

- Pressure groups have the right to organise and meet peacefully without harassment and have the protection of the law. They are entitled to freedom of speech and to raise funds.

- Pressure groups also have a responsibility to obey the law and use only peaceful methods. They must keep accounts for any money they may collect and they must represent the views of the majority of their members. They must also obey the laws that control what can be said, printed or broadcast.

Insider and outsider groups

- According to how closely they work with decision-makers such as governments, councils and other bodies, pressure groups can also be divided into 'insider' and 'outsider' groups. An insider pressure group may be asked to give their opinions on certain issues or give their 'expert' advice to the people making the decisions. Outsider pressure groups will not have these strong links with decision-makers – they will try to exert influence by using the methods below.

EXAM TIP

Research a local pressure group, for example Clydebank Asbestos Action (http://www. clydebankasbestos.org). The examiner will see that you have carried out research and have not relied on the 'usual examples' that many others will use.

Insider groups	Outsider groups
Confederation of British Industry (CBI)	Campaign for Nuclear Disarmament (CND)
The National Farmers' Union (NFU)	The Animal Liberation Front (ALF)
The British Medical Association (BMA)	Fathers for Justice (F4J)

Pressure groups in a democracy

Methods used by pressure groups

In a democracy, pressure groups have the right to use a number of methods that include:

- lobbying elected representatives such as local councillors, MSPs, MPs and MEPs (i.e. trying to 'persuade' them to support the group's ideas)
- running publicity campaigns, e.g. using posters, leaflets, tv adverts, online campaigns and advertisements in the press
- publicity stunts to attract media attention
- boycotting products, shops, companies etc. (boycotting means to stop buying or using a certain product or a certain company)
- writing letters, organising petitions
- protest marches and demonstrations

Advantages of pressure groups

- They put forward the views of people who feel their views are not properly represented by political parties.
- They provide another opportunity for people to participate.
- They can provide information that can 'educate' the public and help them to make more informed decisions.

Disadvantages of pressure groups

- Some pressure groups may only put forward the views of their leaders rather than all of their members.
- Some pressure groups may take actions that are against the law, such as breaking into premises or damaging property.
- As insider groups are not elected, it could be argued that they should not be allowed to influence decision-making.

Quick Test

1. Explain what a pressure group is and what they try to do.
2. What is the difference between sectional and cause groups?
3. Explain what is mean by 'insider' and 'outsider' groups and give some examples.
4. Are pressure groups good or bad for democracy? Give detailed reasons to support your answer.

Trade unions

A trade union is an organisation of workers that tries to protect/improve the working conditions of its members. They also make sure that workplaces are safe and that workers' legal rights are protected. Trade unions represent the views of their members to management, employers and other decision-makers, such as local authorities and governments. Some trade unions also offer their members financial services, such as loans.

Trade unions in the workplace

The role of the shop steward
The diagram below shows the role of the shop steward in the workplace

2. The shop steward negotiates with the management to try to solve disputes between management and workers.

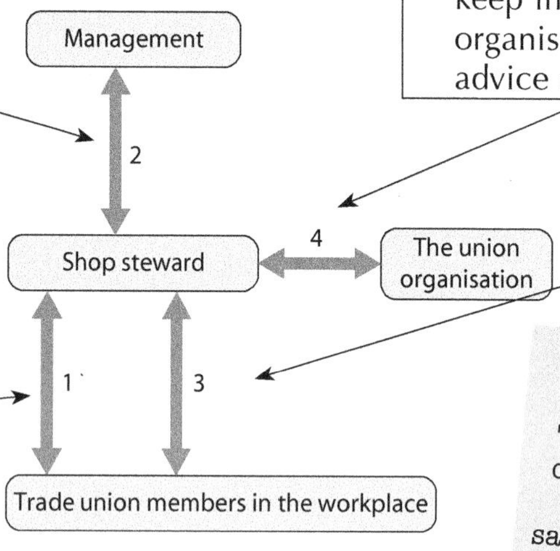

4. The shop steward will also keep in touch with the union organisation to get support and advice on any negotiations.

3. The shop steward passes on the results of these negotiations to the workforce.

1. The union members in the workplace elect a representative. This representative is often known as a **shop steward**.

Management

Shop steward

The union organisation

2

4

1

3

Trade union members in the workplace

EXAM TIP

Trade unions are an example of a sectional pressure group, so remember they have the same rights and responsibilities as pressure groups.

Arguments for joining a trade union
- They negotiate for improved wages and conditions so individual workers do not have to negotiate alone.
- They can prevent individual members from being victimised by their employer.
- They can ensure that workers get their entitlements, such as breaks, minimum pay, holidays etc.
- They make sure the working environment is safe.

Arguments against joining a trade union
- Some people feel they don't need a union if their pay and working conditions are good.
- Some people do not believe in going on strike if it might harm others.
- Some people disagree with the idea of trade unions.

What actions can trade unions take?

Although most disagreements between workers and employers are settled before they get to that stage, unions can take industrial action on behalf of their members in a number of ways.

- **Strikes** – stopping work for a period of time.
- **Work to contract** – doing no tasks other than those in their employment contracts.
- **Overtime bans** – working only the agreed number of hours.

Rights and responsibilities of trade unions and their members

As with pressure groups, trade unions have rights and responsibilities in a democracy.

Rights of trade unions	Responsibilities of trade unions
To organise industrial action.	To ballot their members about an issue (i.e. ask them to vote) and must only use peaceful methods.
To peacefully picket outside their own place of work (persuade other workers to not go in to the workplace).	A maximum of six pickets, who can only use peaceful persuasion.
To operate in a workplace where the majority of the workforce want one.	Unions must allow people to refuse to join or to leave the union.
To negotiate with management on behalf of their members.	To hold elections for important posts in the union, such as shop stewards and general secretaries.

How can individual trade union members participate in their union?

- Attend union meetings to express their views on matters being discussed.
- Stand for one of the elected posts in the union.
- Vote for these elected posts.
- Take part in industrial action when asked to by the union.
- Help to fund the union by paying union fees or dues.

Quick Test

1. What is a trade union and what do they try to do?
2. Describe the role of the shop steward.
3. What opportunities are there for trade union members to take part in the work of their union?
4. Decide whether or not you would choose to join a trade union in the future, giving reasons for your answer.

Poverty and social exclusion in Scotland and the UK

What is poverty?

The most common way that poverty is described is when a person's income is less than the minimum level to meet their basic needs. However, what people mean by 'needs' is different in different parts of the world. That is why organisations like the United Nations refer to absolute poverty and relative poverty.

Absolute poverty – When a person does not have enough resources to meet basic human needs such as food, shelter, warmth, health care etc.

Relative poverty – When some people in a society have a lower income than the average for that society.

Measuring poverty in the UK

Although there is some disagreement about how to 'measure' poverty, it can be argued that, in the UK, poorer sections of society are more likely to be in relative poverty rather than absolute poverty. Relative poverty in the UK is defined as a household income that is less than 60% of the median income, which means that households below that income are excluded from living the kind of life that is 'normal' for people in that society.

Poverty and social exclusion

One of the main effects of poverty is social exclusion. To be 'excluded' means to be left out of something. Social exclusion is when individuals, groups of people or areas suffer from a combination of problems caused by poverty, which can 'exclude' them from having the same opportunities as others to take part in the social, political and economic life of the country. The Poverty and Social Exclusion research organisation (www.poverty.ac.uk) says that poverty and social exclusion are so closely linked that you cannot talk about one without the other.

Groups likely to be affected most

This unit will look at different groups in the population who are more likely to be affected by poverty and social exclusion. Remember that this does *not* mean that all members of that group will be affected. These groups include the elderly, ethnic minorities, women, lone parent families, and people with physical and mental needs.

Poverty in Scotland

In March 2018, Scottish Government figures on poverty in Scotland showed that:

- Poverty rates in Scotland are continuing to rise.
- In each year between 2014 and 2017, one million people in Scotland were living in poverty, which was up slightly on previous years.
- Poverty rates for single adult women were higher than for single adult men, whether or not they had children.
- Poverty rates for minority ethnic groups were higher than for the white ethnic group.
- Poverty rates for families with a disabled member were higher than for families without.
- 24% of children (230,000) were living in relative poverty during the period 2014–17, up 1% on 2013–16.
- 13% of pensioners (140,000) were living in relative poverty, up 1% on the previous three-year period.

EXAM TIP

Information about poverty can go out of date quickly. Organisations such as The Poverty Alliance publish regular reports with up-to-date figures. They publish information specifically about Scotland, as well as the UK. Examiners will expect recent, relevant examples.

Quick Test

1. Explain the difference between relative poverty and absolute poverty.
2. Explain the meaning of the social exclusion diagram.
3. Which groups of people in society are more likely to be affected by poverty and social exclusion?
4. What evidence is there to support this in the Scottish Government's figures?

The causes of poverty

There are many causes of poverty and social exclusion. Some individuals, groups and areas are affected by several of these causes.

Low pay

In the UK, the National Minimum Wage and the National Living Wage (NMW and NLW) set by the government mean that employers must pay their workers a minimum hourly rate according to age. However, according to organisations such as The Living Wage Foundation, the NMW and NLW are less than a 'real living wage based on what people need to live'. They claim that the 'real living wage' should be at least £1 per hour more. The Living Wage Foundation states that over 6 million workers earn less than this 'real living wage'.

National Minimum Wage Rates | National Living Wage

2018

£3.70 — Apprentice Rate
£4.20 — 16–17 yrs
£5.90 — 18–20 yrs
£7.38 — 21–24 yrs
£7.83 — 25 yrs+

The benefits system

If people are unable to work or have incomes below a certain level, then in the UK there are a number of benefits they might be entitled to. These benefits are described in detail on page 52. Ever since the financial crash in 2007, governments have tried to make savings in the amount of money spent on benefits. In 2018 the government made a number of changes including:

- A four-year 'cash freeze' on working age benefits was continued.
- Child benefit only available for the first two children.
- A 'cap' or limit on the maximum amount of benefits a family can get per week. In 2018 this was £384.62 per week for couples and lone parents outside Greater London.

Unemployment

At the time this book was written, the unemployment rate in the UK was 4.3%, meaning that for every 100 people who are able to work and looking for work, more than 4 were not working. For most people, their main income comes from the wages or salary they earn from their job, and therefore unemployment is one of the main causes of poverty. According to research by the Joseph Rowntree Foundation, of all the things that caused people to 'escape from poverty', the top three reasons involved people in a household getting a job or getting a better job. In fact, their research showed that 7 in 10 people who are in poverty move out of poverty when they get a full-time job.

Gender and race

This section of the book will focus on women and ethnic minorities in some detail as they are more likely to experience poverty than other sections of society. The Joseph Rowntree Foundation states that 'women are, and have always been, more likely to experience poverty than men'. In 2018, 5.2 million women were in poverty compared to 4.7 million men and overall, people from the Asian, Black and Other ethnic groups are more likely to live in low income households, with 18% of Asian people and 16% of Black people living in low income households compared with 9% of White British people.

Area

Every four years, the Scottish government publishes the Scottish Index of Multiple Deprivation (SIMD). In both 2012 and 2016 it listed Ferguslie Park in Renfrewshire as the most deprived area of Scotland. Seven of the ten most deprived areas in Scotland are in Glasgow City. There are many reasons for this, including high levels of unemployment, lower levels of educational attainment, higher levels of poor health, crime and substance abuse.

Family structure

In modern Britain there are many different types of family structure, including couples with children, lone parents, extended families etc. Statistically, certain family types are more likely to be affected by poverty:

- lone parent families – around half of lone parent families have a low income
- reconstituted families, where one or both parents have children from a previous relationship
- families where no adult is in employment
- families that are headed by a teenage parent
- families that have a child under 5 years of age
- families that have a disabled child
- families that have a large number of children

EXAM TIP

Although some types of family are more likely than others to experience poverty, you must *never* stereotype that type of family. For example, not all lone parent families rely on benefits.

Quick Test

1. Explain the difference between the National Living Wage and the 'real living wage'.
2. What evidence is there that having a job is important in 'escaping poverty'?
3. Which types of family are most likely to have a low income?
4. Why are some areas poorer than others?

The effects of poverty

There are many problems that poorer people are more likely to experience, as this diagram shows.

Poorer health

The effects of poverty on health are serious and often lifelong. Children born into poor households are more likely to:

- be born early (premature) and have a low birth weight, which can cause problems later in life
- die before their first birthday (sudden infant death syndrome occurs nine times more often in the poorest families compared with the richest families)
- miss more school days because of poor health

Mental health

According to the Scottish Public Health Observatory, 'Major risk factors for mental health problems include poverty, poor education, unemployment, social isolation/exclusion and major life events'. Adults in the poorest group in society are much more likely to be at risk of developing a mental illness than those on average incomes. This does not mean that poverty causes mental illness, but poorer people are more likely to live in areas with many social problems such as drugs, violence and poor housing. They are also likely to suffer more stress. These things can cause poor mental health. Also, people who do have mental health problems are more likely to be unemployed, so they may be forced to live in poorer areas.

Substance misuse

Poverty by itself does not lead to people misusing alcohol and drugs. However, although there is not much difference between the percentage of young people from different social classes who experiment with drugs, people from the poorest sections of society are more likely to use drugs more often and are more likely to become addicted. This also applies to alcohol. According to Alcohol Focus Scotland, people from the poorest areas of Scotland are eight times more likely to be admitted to hospital with alcohol-related problems than people from better-off areas.

Education

In recent years in Scotland there has been an increase in the number of students from poorer areas gaining a university place. In 2017 it reached its highest level ever, of 4,150 students from poorer areas. However, this was only 14% of the total number of university students, which means that the well-off are still far more likely to attend university. What are the reasons for this? Many studies have shown that the education of children from the poorest households will be affected by things such as:

- being less likely to live in a household that encourages learning, especially at a young age – this includes things like parents encouraging them to learn, having a quiet place to study, having books in the home, etc.
- being more likely to miss schooling as a result of absences caused by poor health or exclusions for poor behaviour
- their school being in an area of multiple deprivation, which means they are less likely to achieve good grades or go on to university

Housing and area

According to the Joseph Ronwntree foundation, the gap between the poorest and richest areas in the UK is getting bigger. Although it is very important not to 'stereotype' people living in deprived areas such as Ferguslie Park, Possil Park and Keppoch, which are among the poorest areas in Scotland, they are more likely to suffer from problems such as:

- lack of opportunities for employment
- lack of role models for young people
- crime and gangs
- substance misuse
- antisocial behaviour
- lack of amenities

Antisocial behavior is more common in deprived areas

Although poor families are more likely to live in local authority or 'council housing,' the housing pressure group Shelter estimates that almost 25% of families in Scotland could be 'one pay cheque away from losing their homes', which shows that people who are buying their homes are also facing housing problems as a result of losing their jobs or not having enough money to pay for their basic needs and their mortgage.

Quick Test

1. In what ways can poverty affect the lives of children born into poorer households?
2. Why do fewer pupils from poorer backgrounds gain a place in university?
3. Describe the type of problems facing people living in Scotland's poorest areas.
4. What is the connection between poverty and addiction?

Tackling poverty: 1

In Scotland and the rest of the UK, there are various organisations and schemes aimed at tackling poverty.

The UK Government

EXAM TIP

For a more detailed list of benefits, including the current amounts paid, visit the website of the Department for Work and Pensions (DWP).

The UK is a welfare state, which means that there are a range of benefits and payments to help people when they are unemployed, sick or have an income below a certain level. There are also schemes to help vulnerable groups, such as children, disabled people and the elderly.

There is a wide variety of benefits. Some of the main benefits and schemes are shown in this table.

Universal Credit	When it is fully introduced, this will be a single benefit payment that replaces a range of benefits. It is aimed at people who are looking for work or are in work but on a low income.
Child Benefit	Paid to families if they have a child or children under 16 (or under 20 in education) if their income is below a certain level.
Tax Credits	Tax-free state benefits to provide extra money to people responsible for children, to disabled workers and other workers on lower incomes. The two main types are Working Tax Credits and Child Tax Credits.
Jobseeker's Allowance	Jobseeker's Allowance is a benefit for people who are not in full-time employment (work less than 16 hours per week), are capable of working and are looking for work.
The National Minimum Wage and the National Living Wage	These set the minimum amount per hour that employers must pay their workers. The amount paid will depend on the age of the worker or if they are an apprentice.
State Pensions	This is paid to anyone who has reached retirement and has paid enough into the state pension scheme to qualify.
Winter Fuel Allowance and Cold Weather Payment	An amount between £100 and £300 paid to anyone born before 1953 who is also receiving the state pension. Some older people may also qualify for a Cold Weather Payment if the temperature falls below freezing for over 7 days.
Other family benefits include	Maternity Grants, Childcare Grants and free school meals.

Welfare to work – getting people into work

The most important way to get out of poverty is through employment. The UK government has introduced a number of schemes to get people to move from welfare to work. *Get Britain Working* is the title of the government welfare to work policy. It consists of several schemes, including:

- **Work Clubs** – Local groups of volunteers who get together to encourage people who are out of work to share skills and experience to help find a job. They provide unemployed people with a place to meet and exchange skills.

- **Work Experience** – Aimed at young people aged 16–24 who are first-time job seekers or who have had problems getting a job. They can work for an employer unpaid for 2–8 weeks while still receiving their benefits. The aim is to gain the kind of skills and experience needed to get a job.

- **The Work and Health Programme** – Provides support to help people find and keep a job. It is voluntary for people with a health condition or disability. It is compulsory for those unemployed for over two years. It will replace the Work Programme and Work Choice programmes in 2018.

- **New Enterprise Allowance** – Provides support to unemployed people who want to start their own business. Participants are supported by volunteer business mentors and can apply for financial support once they start their business.

- **Jobcentre Plus** – Many of these schemes are run by Jobcentre Plus. The main purpose of Jobcentre Plus is to help people to find work. It keeps a database of jobs in the local area, nationally and abroad and can help to arrange interviews. It gives information and advice about benefits, organises skill training and helps people to complete application forms and CVs. In order to qualify for Jobseeker's Allowance, people out of work must register with a Jobcentre Plus.

Most towns have a Jobcentre Plus

Quick Test

1. What is meant by a welfare state?
2. From the table of benefits, select the three that you think are the most important. Give reasons for your choices.
3. Explain what the phrase 'welfare to work' means.
4. Describe the part played by volunteers in some of the employment schemes described above.

Tackling poverty: 2

Poverty in Scotland – *The Fairer Scotland Action Plan*

Since devolution, the Scottish Parliament has had responsibility for many areas of policy that can affect poverty and social exclusion. The Scottish Government's strategy to tackle poverty and social exclusion in Scotland are set out in *The Fairer Scotland Action Plan*, which sets out five main 'ambitions' for the period up to 2030, including a fairer Scotland for all, ending child poverty, a strong start for all young people, fairer working lives and improving the lives of older people.

Recent policies in Scotland

Since the opening of the modern Scottish Parliament in 2009, there have been several important policies aimed at reducing inequality including:

- **The abolition of prescription charges**. In 2011, the Scottish Parliament passed a law abolishing payments for prescriptions. All prescriptions for medicines are now free in Scotland. The same is true in Wales and Northern Ireland. It was argued that this would keep more people out of hospital and would save money in the long run.

First Minister Nicola Sturgeon

- **Free personal care for the elderly**. Since the passing of the Community Care and Health Act in 2002, elderly people in Scotland can get help in their homes with things such a personal hygiene, help with medication, mobility etc.

- **The abolition of tuition fees**. Since the year 2000, Scottish students do not have to pay tuition fees to attend university. It was hoped that this would encourage more students from poorer backgrounds.

- **Free early education and childcare**. In 2018, the parents of children aged 3–4 in Scotland are entitled to 16 hours per week free early learning and childcare. The Scottish Government has stated that this will double by 2020. This service allows parents more opportunities to work and aims to improve life chances for disadvantaged and vulnerable children.

Scottish students do not pay tuition fees

- **More Choices, More Chances (MCMC).** In Scotland in 2017, according to Scottish Government figures, almost 9% of 16–19 year olds were not in education, employment and training (NEET). The MCMC policy tries to make sure school leavers are given help and advice to continue their education or find a job or training.

- **Scotland's Regeneration Strategy**. This is the Scottish Government's plan to improve and regenerate some of Scotland's most deprived communities. Funding is made available to improve the areas, help local businesses and encourage other businesses to set up in these areas. In 2018, for example, £26 million was made available to various projects such as a £4 million grant to refurbish Paisley museum.

- **Scottish Living Wage Scheme.** The Scottish Government encourages employers to pay more than the legal minimum wage of £7.83 in 2018. Employers who take part in the Scottish Living Wage Scheme agree to pay employees £8.75 and in return they are 'accredited' and can promote their business as a Real Living Wage Employer.

- **Scottish Enterprise and Highlands and Islands Enterprise.** Offer help to existing and new businesses in Scotland to grow and take on more workers. They do this by giving business advice, help with skills training, developing products and helping to find premises.

> **EXAM TIP**
>
> Remember that some of the policies described here may only apply to Scotland, for example in other parts of the UK prescriptions are still paid for as is personal care for the elderly, and students in England in 2018 may have to pay fees of more than £9,000 per year.

The work of charities and voluntary groups

In the UK there are very many charities and voluntary groups that try to reduce poverty and social exclusion. Organisations such as the Child Poverty Action Group and Barnardo's do this in a number of ways

Quick Test

1. What are the main aims of *The Fairer Scotland Action Plan*?
2. Describe how the Scottish Enterprise and Highlands and Islands Enterprise try to create jobs.
3. Which policies show the importance of education in tackling poverty?
4. How might free early education and childcare reduce poverty and inequality?

Health inequality

Scotland's health

In 2017, the *Herald* newspaper reported on the health divide in Scotland between the poor and the better off. It stated that:

- The health gap between the poorest and richest Scots is widening.
- The poorest in society are much more likely to die from alcohol abuse, coronary heart disease and cancer.
- The better off make more use of cancer screening programmes and are likely to have cancer detected at an early stage.
- The poorest Scots were 3.7 times more likely to die early than the better off (up from 2.7 in 1997).
- In the 15–44 age group, which has the highest rates of suicide, assault and drug overdoses, the poorest were six times more likely to die than the richest.
- Men are more likely to die of preventable diseases than women.

When asked about the reasons for this, Dr Gerry McCartney, the Head of Public Health Observatory at NHS Health Scotland stated: 'For wealthy countries like Scotland, socio-economic inequalities are the most important factor in determining the extent of health inequalities.'

However, although Scotland is sometimes called 'The Sick Man of Europe', according to the Office for National Statistics, there have been health improvements in Scotland in the 10 years up to 2017:

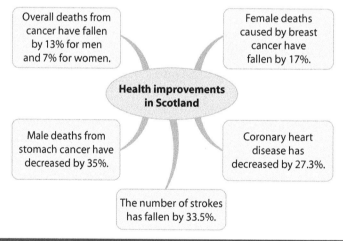

Overall deaths from cancer have fallen by 13% for men and 7% for women.

Female deaths caused by breast cancer have fallen by 17%.

Health improvements in Scotland

Male deaths from stomach cancer have decreased by 35%.

Coronary heart disease has decreased by 27.3%.

The number of strokes has fallen by 33.5%.

Tackling health inequalities

As health is a devolved issue, most of the policies affecting the health of people in Scotland are decided by the Scottish Parliament. The Scottish Government's 'A Fairer Healthier Scotland 2017–22' action plan aims to:

- increase physical activity
- improve mental wellbeing
- reduce premature mortality
- reduce the percentage of adults who smoke
- reduce alcohol-related hospital admissions
- reduce the number of individuals with problem drug use

As part of this programme of health improvement, a number of policies have been introduced.

A ban on smoking in public places	In March 2006, smoking in enclosed or mostly enclosed public spaces was banned. Scottish smoking rates have fallen from 31% in 2003 to 21% in 2015.
A minimum price for alcohol	In May of 2018, the Scottish Parliament set a minimum price on a unit of alcohol to try to reduce alcohol-related health problems. People in Scotland drink 20% more alcohol than in the rest of the UK.
School meals	All children in Primary 1–3 are entitled to free school meals. There are strict standards for the nutritional value of food and drink served in schools. Just under half of pupils in Scottish schools have a school lunch.
Free prescriptions	Since 2011, people in Scotland do not pay for prescriptions.
Compulsory PE and *Active Schools*	Schools must provide 2 hours of physical activity per week. The *Active Schools* programme employs specialist staff to provide sports opportunities for pupils during and after the school day.
Well man and Well woman clinics	Clinics aimed at providing a wide range of health check-ups and advice for men and women can be found in some hospitals and GP surgeries, and in some private clinics.
Curriculum for Excellence	Health and Wellbeing is a central part of the Scottish curriculum. Pupils learn about the importance of healthy living and healthy choices, among other things.
Health campaigns	Examples include *See Me*, to improve mental health awareness, and *Take it Right Outside*, to encourage smokers to smoke outdoors if there are others in the house.

EXAM TIP

Although Scotland may be called the 'Sick Man of Europe,' if Glasgow, Inverclyde, West Dunbartonshire and Dundee were taken out of Scotland's health figures, Scotland would have similar health to the rest of Europe.

Quick Test

1. Apart from poverty, which other factors can affect health?
2. What name that is sometimes given to Scotland suggests it has poorer health than elsewhere?
3. What are the main aims of 'A Fairer Healthier Scotland'?
4. Which policies in the table above show the importance of focusing on children and young people?

Ethnic inequality

The ethnic population of the UK

Historically, Scotland has always been a multicultural society. The Scottish people were a combination of Picts, Gaels, Britons, Anglo-Saxons and Norse! Today, Scotland continues to be a multicultural and multiethnic society. People classed as Black, Asian and Minority Ethnic (BAME) make up just over 2% of the total Scottish population. Of that population:

- Pakistanis are the largest minority ethnic group, followed by Chinese, Indians and those of mixed ethnic backgrounds

- over 70% of the total ethnic minority population are Asian: Indian, Pakistani, Bangladeshi, Chinese or other South Asian

- over 12% of the minority ethnic population are of mixed ethnicity

- the BAME group is growing faster than the general population

- the BAME percentage of the population of Scotland is smaller than in the rest of the UK

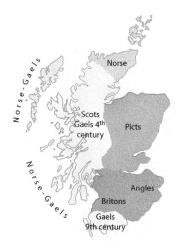

In England and Wales, the 2011 census shows that:

- ethnic Whites make up 86% of the total population (it had been 91.3% in 2001)

- people of Irish and Polish origin are the biggest category of foreign-born residents

- Indians are the largest non-White group, closely followed by Pakistanis

- 12% of households are 'mixed,' i.e. comprised of people from different ethnic or national groups

- more people are classifying themselves as 'mixed' ethnicity

- the BAME groups and more recently arrived immigrant groups are growing faster than the general population

- BAME groups are more concentrated in urban areas, especially deprived areas

- BAME groups are becoming less segregated in where they live

However, certain trends can be seen for some members of BAME groups:

- poverty rates are higher

- wages are lower, even among university graduates

- they are less likely to be promoted

- unemployment is higher

- educational attainment is lower

- conviction rates for crime are higher

- they are more likely to be stopped, searched or arrested than White people

- overall health is poorer

EXAM TIP

Do not think of people of BAME backgrounds as a single group. In fact some of the inequalities between different BAME groups are greater than the inequality between BAME groups and the White population. For example, people of Black, Pakistani and Caribbean origin are at higher risk of inequality than other groups, while Indians, Chinese and Asians do well in the education system.

What are the reasons for ethnic inequality?

We have already seen that poverty and social exclusion can be caused by a number of factors. These will apply to different groups, but have more effect in some groups than others.

- Most BAME groups live in cities. Many live in poor, run-down areas with poor schooling.
- Some may not have English as a first language at home.
- They experience prejudice and discrimination among employers and other organisations.
- There are fewer job opportunities in the areas where they live.
- They have fewer or no qualifications.

The Equality Act 2010

You will read elsewhere in the book about various policies that try to reduce inequality in health and income, and these will apply to BAME groups as well; however, there are certain laws that are aimed specifically at preventing discrimination of certain groups, including women and BAME groups. In 2010, the UK government passed the  Equality Act, which makes it illegal to discriminate against people because of age, race, gender, gender reassignment, sexual orientation, marital status, pregnancy and maternity or disability.

The Act states that no one should be discriminated against because of these characteristics in employment, the provision of goods and services and education and in all government organisations, such as councils.

Quick Test

1. Why can it be said that Scotland is a multicultural nation now and was a multicultural nation in the past?
2. What evidence is there of BAME group inequality?
3. Explain the main causes of this inequality.
4. Summarise the main points of the Equality Act 2010.

Ethnic inequality: employment

Employment inequality – an overview

When Theresa May became Prime Minister in 2106, she gave a speech in which she described the results of a Race Disparity Audit that she had ordered to be carried out. In her speech she said that the report showed the difficulties facing certain groups in society, including people from a BAME background. This situation is not a new one for the UK, where employment inequality affects most BAME groups more than others.

In May of 2018, a House of Commons Briefing paper on 'Unemployment by Ethnic Background' showed a clear difference in unemployment rates between White and BAME groups:

- Unemployment among Whites was 3.8% compared with 7.1% for people from the BAME groups.
- The unemployment rate is highest for people from a Bangladeshi background, at 12%.
- 10% of people from Pakistani or Black backgrounds were unemployed.
- Youth unemployment for Bangladeshi and Pakistani young people is more than double the rate for Whites.

In promoted posts, the Chartered Management Institute showed in 2017 that only 6% of promoted posts were held by BAME groups – less than half their percentage in the workplace. And in 2017, the 'Race at Work' report showed there is a large difference in the employment rates between White women (72.6%) compared to BAME women (55.8%). When Tidjanie Thiam was appointed in 2009, he was the first ever Black Chief Executive Officer of one of Britain's top 100 companies.

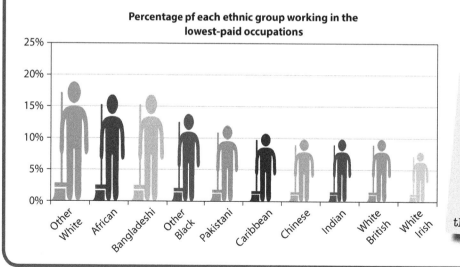

Percentage pf each ethnic group working in the lowest-paid occupations

EXAM TIP

The Equalities and Human Rights Commission states that complaints about racial and ethnic prejudice in the workplace make up a large percentage of the cases they deal with.

Employment patterns of BME groups

A recent survey by the Institute for Employment Research found that there tended to be more people from the BAME groups in some jobs than others. It also found that there was a lower percentage of BAME workers in the best-paid jobs.

| BAME employment patterns by job type ||
Under-represented	Over-represented
Managers and administrators	Machine and transport operatives
Professionals (e.g. lawyers, accountants)	Sales
Skilled manual	Health and social work
Construction	Food, drink and tobacco

Why is this the case?
- BAME groups are more likely to live in deprived areas where there are fewer job opportunities and higher unemployment.
- There are fewer promotion opportunities in many of the types of occupations with a higher percentage of BAME members.
- Some professions are seen by BAME groups as 'less welcoming' according to the Race for Opportunity report. People from BAME groups are less likely to apply for professions such as the police and legal professions.
- For some BAME group members, particularly older members, language may be a barrier to getting a job if they do not speak English as their first language.
- Spending cuts by councils and organisations like the NHS affect BAME groups more as a higher percentage are employed in government-funded jobs than in other types of jobs.

An improving situation
In the 2015 report *How Fair is Britain* published by the Equality and Human Rights Commission every five years, it states that, while there is still a significant gap between BAME groups and Whites when it comes to employment, there have been some improvements, for example:
- Indian and Chinese people in Britain are twice as likely to be employed as professionals as White British people and the trend is upwards
- Muslim men are as likely to be in managerial/professional jobs as unskilled jobs
- since 1995, the percentage of Bangladeshi and Pakistani people in work has increased by three times the average
- Black-Caribbean and Bangladeshi pupils have begun to catch up with the average performance at GCSE, increasing their job opportunities

Quick Test

1. Explain why the appointment of Tidjanie Thiam can be described as 'unusual'.
2. Give three pieces of evidence that BAME groups face greater employment inequality than Whites.
3. What evidence is there that some BAME groups face greater inequality than others?
4. Give three reasons why this inequality continues.

Ethnic inequality: health

Generally speaking, BAME groups have worse health than the overall population of the United Kingdom. Within the BAME population, some groups have worse health than others and are affected by different health conditions.

Health inequality among BAME groups

- Some BAME groups have worse health than others:
  - Pakistani, Bangladeshi and Black-Caribbean people have the poorest health
  - Asians and Black Africans have similar health to Whites
  - Chinese people have better health than the general population
  - for some BAME groups, the health of those born in the UK is worse than first-generation immigrants in that group
- Young Asian women are twice as likely to commit suicide as young White women.
- People of Indian origin are three times more likely to have diabetes.
- BAME groups have more heart disease but fewer cancers than the White population.

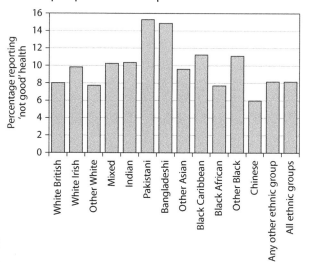

What are the causes of health inequality?

- **Poverty and social exclusion.** All studies show that while there might be some factors that affect the health of some groups more than others, the factor with the biggest impact on health is poverty and social exclusion.
- **Housing and area.** Most new immigrant populations will settle in inner-city areas where poverty and deprivation already exist. Poor-quality housing and overcrowding leads to more disease than in better-off areas.
- **Employment**. Often immigrant groups have to take the jobs that are lower paid, unhealthy and dangerous.
- **Culture**. Some BAME groups are more affected by lifestyle choices than others, for example South Asians:
  - have higher levels of saturated fat in their diet, e.g. ghee
  - have higher levels of smoking among males
  - take less exercise

- **Biology**. Some evidence suggests that certain groups are more likely to suffer from certain diseases, for example people of African, African-Caribbean, Asian or Mediterranean origin are more likely to suffer from a blood disorder called sickle cell anaemia. Also, men born in South Asia are 50% more likely to have a heart attack or angina than men in the general population.
- **Mental Health**. People of Black-Caribbean and African origin are more than seven times more likely to come into contact with mental health services. Part of the reason for this is, again, the lifestyle caused by poverty and social exclusion, but also many people are referred to mental health services by the prison and court system. People of Black-Caribbean and African origin are more likely to be arrested and imprisoned.

Policies to reduce health inequality

The Equality Act 2010
The Equality Act 2010, which is dealt with in more detail elsewhere in the book, makes it illegal for people in the UK to be discriminated against because of such things as race and gender. It also means that access to things like health care must be fair and open to all.

Race for Health
In England and Wales the NHS has made a 'pledge' to reduce race inequality in the four main areas of diabetes, mental health, childbirth deaths and coronary heart disease and stroke. They also pledge to implement race equality legislation, to improve services and to improve the race equality performance of the NHS as an employer.

A Fairer Healthier Scotland
A Fairer Healthier Scotland is the Scottish Government's plan to reduce health inequalities. It aims to deal with the underlying causes of poor health, such as poverty, unemployment and poor living conditions.

NHS Scotland Equality Outcomes Plan 2013–17
Equality Outcomes state what the Scottish Government plans to do in different areas of Scottish life. One of these outcomes is to improve health for all groups in society, including people from different ethnic groups, making sure that no groups would be 'left behind in terms of health improvement and reduction of health inequalities'.

Quick Test

1. What is the main factor that has the biggest impact on health inequality among BAME groups?
2. What evidence is there that some groups in the population have worse health than others? Refer to the graph on page 62 in your answer.
3. Why are people of Black-Caribbean and African origin more likely to come into contact with mental health services than other groups?
4. What attempts have been made in the UK to tackle health inequalities?

Gender inequality: employment

Successful women

Of the main free-to-air channels in the UK, two of them, Channel 4 and ITV are led by women. Dame Carolyn McCall became head of ITV in 2017. She had previously been head of easyJet for seven years. In that same year, Alex Mahon was appointed as the Chief Executive Officer of Channel 4.

Increasing numbers of women like Carolyn McCall are becoming successful not only in business but in many other professions. For example:

Dame Carolyn McCall, head of ITV

- in 2017, a record number of 208 women were elected to the UK Parliament
- between 2009 and 2017, the number of female board members in Britain's top 100 companies almost doubled
- girls of all ethnic groups are out-performing boys at all levels in school and are 37% more likely to go to university than men
- there are now more female judges than ever before
- the average wage gap between men and women has fallen steadily in recent years

However, although women have made progress, it should be remembered that despite having laws to try to reduce gender inequality (some going back to the 1970s), the average pay gap between men and women in the UK today is still around 15%. This is one of the highest in Europe. The Trade Union Congress has stated it will take the UK 40 years to achieve equal pay between men and women if the pay gap reduces at its present rate. In 2017, the Women and Equalities committee reported that the UK had fallen from 25th in 1999 to 48th position in the world for women in parliaments. In business, out of Britain's top 100 companies, only seven have female Chief Executive Officers. Even in those areas where women are strongly represented such as secondary education, in Scotland, 65% of teachers are women, but only 41% are headteachers.

The glass ceiling

From the evidence, it is clear than that there are barriers in the way of many women being appointed to top jobs. This is sometimes called the 'glass ceiling' because women (and other groups such as minorities and disabled people) can see the jobs they want to go for but in many cases they are not successful. It is as though an invisible barrier is preventing them from being successful.

The reasons for continued gender inequality

Reason	Explanation
The glass ceiling	Although top jobs are 'officially' open to women, there are fewer women than you might expect in these jobs. Some say there is an 'invisible' barrier – a 'glass ceiling' that stops women from getting to the top.
Childcare	Women with children may find it more difficult to take a full-time job or a job that involves unsocial hours or travelling away from home.
Stereotyping and discrimination	Some employers may have a stereotyped view of the work that men and women should do, and may not choose women for certain jobs.
The four 'Cs'	Women tend to be concentrated in certain jobs such as the so-called 'four Cs' – catering, cleaning, caring and cashier work. These jobs tend to be less skilled and less well-paid.
Part-time work	There are three times as many women part-time workers as men. They are often lower paid, most likely to lose their jobs if there is a downturn in the economy and their jobs less likely to lead to promotion.
Career breaks	Women who take a break in their careers to have children may find it difficult to return to work at the same position, as they may have to cut back on the hours they can work and they may find their skills are outdated.

EXAM TIP

When you are answering questions in the exam you will be expected to support your points with relevant and up-to-date examples. As you study and revise, you should 'collect' examples from a variety of different sources, e.g. newspapers, television news and the Internet. Your examples must come from reliable sources, such as the BBC or government websites. Take notes of the key points, the source of the example and the date.

Quick Test

1. Draw up a table like the one below and complete it using the information in this section.

Evidence of female progress	Evidence of continued female inequality

2. Explain why so many women in the workforce are in part-time jobs.

3. What is meant by 'the glass ceiling'?

Gender inequality: health

Evidence of gender health differences

Gender is one of the factors that can cause health inequality. In most counties, male life expectancy is lower than female life expectancy and this gap is predicted to continue, although it is beginning to get smaller. In the UK, according to the Office for National Statistics, a boy born today can expect to live to 79 while a girl can expect to live to just over 82.

- Men are four times more likely to commit suicide than women.
- Women have a higher rate of illness than men.
- Women go to the doctors more often than men.
- Women are more likely to suffer depression or mental illness than men.
- Men are twice as likely to die from the ten most common cancers as women.
- The Scottish Health Survey 2016 showed that men were significantly more likely than women to be overweight, including obese, in 2016 (68% compared with 61%).

Why do women live longer than men?

Lifestyle choices

Men tend to make poorer lifestyle choices than women, for example:

- men smoke more than women – there is only a 3% difference according to the Office for National Statistics; however, more men smoke unfiltered or hand-rolled cigarettes

- men drink more than women – in Scotland there are over twice as many male as female alcohol-related deaths

- men do not go to the doctors as much as women – a survey of 1,000 men for Men's Health Week 2017 showed that three-quarters will put off going to the doctors when showing signs of illness

Men make poorer lifestyle choices

- men are more likely to take part in risky and dangerous activities, such as driving fast; the Department of Transport figures show that, overall, around seven of every 10 people killed or seriously injured in road accidents are male

- men are more likely to be involved in violence; two-thirds (68%) of homicide victims are male

- women are less likely to take part in a sporting activity; the Women in Sport organisation reported in 2018 that only 8% of girls are doing the recommended amount of weekly exercise

Occupation

Traditionally, men tend to do more dangerous jobs and are more likely than women to be killed or injured at work. Men are more likely to:

- work at heights
- use heavy equipment and power tools
- come into contact with dangerous materials such as asbestos

Health and Safety Executive figures show that in 2017/18, 138 (96%) of all workplace deaths were male. The three occupations with the most deaths tend to attract far more men than women:

- construction
- farming
- waste recycling

Biology

Although the main causes of poor health affect both men and women – heart disease and cancer – there are certain conditions thaat affect one gender more than the other:

- twice as many women as men die from dementia and Alzheimer's (probably due to their longer lifespan)
- certain cancers affect one gender more than the other:
  - prostate cancer affects only men and in the UK is the most common cancer among men
  - breast cancer is a disease that affects women far more than men (only 1% of breast cancer patients are male)
- some scientists are now suggesting that differences in the biological make-up of male and female cells may play a part in women living longer than men

Gender, health and poverty

One of the most important factors that affect male and female health is poverty. For example, the *British Journal of Cancer* found that poorer women have a 6% lower chance of surviving breast cancer than better-off women and they have a higher rate of cervical cancer. Men in poor areas have a worse chance of surviving cancers. One of the reasons for this is that people from poorer backgrounds are less likely to go for check-ups and tests, or they go to the doctor at a later stage of the disease. Less well-off people are also more likely to make poor lifestyle choices.

Quick Test

1. What evidence is there of health differences between men and women?
2. How might occupation affect the health of men and women differently?
3. Explain what is meant by 'risky activities' and what evidence is there that men are more likely than women to do these?
4. How can biology affect health?

The Government of China

Background

Since 1949, when they defeated the old Chinese government in a civil war, the Communist Party of China (CPC) has totally dominated all aspects of life in China, even though many of the 'key features' of democracy described in the chapters on India and the USA are contained in the Chinese Constitution. 'Guaranteed' rights include: the right to vote, freedom of speech, religious freedom, the right to protest, a free media.

However, there are also responsibilities or 'duties' that the Chinese people are expected to fulfil:

- abide by the laws of the People's Republic of China
- protect public property
- observe labour discipline (in reality this is discouraging workers from taking industrial action)
- protect state secrets
- safeguard the honour, security and interests of the motherland

The reality is that the CPC does not allow any real opposition and controls these rights very strictly, as you will see later in this chapter.

EXAM TIP

Information on many countries, including China, can be found on the BBC Country Profiles website where you can find background information on the politics, economics and history of China. This website is regularly updated so is very useful when looking for examples to support the points you make in knowledge and understanding questions in the course assessments.

The Chinese Communist Party

- It is claimed that there are over 80 million members of the CPC, which makes it the biggest political party in the world.
- The CPC has controlled and dominated all aspects of life in China for over six decades, including:
  - what people are allowed to read, watch and say
  - all aspects of the school and university curriculum
  - how many children Chinese families are allowed

Membership of the CPC is sought by many people because they see it as the best way to make sure they 'get on' in life. However, some groups find it harder to get in than others. It is mostly male – only around 25% of members are female – and it tends to consist of people such as government workers, officers in the armed forces as well as farmers and so-called 'model workers' who are meant to be an example to others. In order to be accepted, people who apply must:

- be nominated by existing Party members
- undergo very rigorous background checks to make sure they are 'suitable'
- undertake a year's probation, where they must undertake training and even more 'checks'

The domination of the CPC

The control that the CPC has over decision-making in China can be seen by looking at the way China is governed. In democracies such as the UK, the USA and India, political parties may be in 'control' of the government because that party won an election, but this 'control' ends if they are defeated in a later election. The situation is quite different in China as this diagram shows. In other words, although on paper the Chinese Government and the Chinese Communist Party are separate, in fact it is the Party that makes all the decisions about what should happen in almost all aspects of life in China.

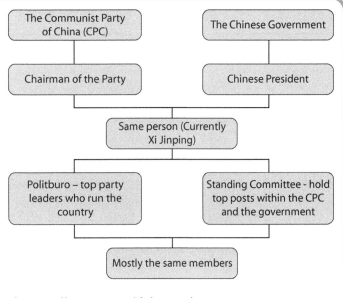

The Parliament of China (NPC)

The Parliament of China is called the National People's Congress (NPC). It is made up of almost 3000 members called 'delegates' who are elected every 5 years. There is a much smaller group of delegates called the 'Standing Committee' of the NPC. This committee has the power to make laws and change the Chinese Constitution. In fact, because most of the members of the Committee are members of the CPC, it is really the Party that makes the decisions.

The Politburo

The Politburo is the main decision-making body in China. It is made up of 24 members. Within the Politburo, however, there is a smaller committee called the 'Standing Committee'. This is a very secretive group and the outside world very rarely gets to finds out what goes on. It is not elected. Once this committee takes a decision, all of the members, even if they disagreed in private, must support the decisions. The Standing Committee also decides who will be given the top jobs in the CPC and the government.

China's (all male) Standing Committee of the Politburo

Quick Test

1. In what ways does the CPC dominate all aspects of Chinese life?
2. Explain how the CPC also controls the government of China.
3. Describe the membership of the Party and the process new members have to go through.
4. Explain the importance of the Standing Committee of the Politburo.

How democratic is China?

In order to answer this question, it is necessary to ask whether or not China shows the same 'key features' of a democracy as outlined in the chapters on India and the USA.

Regular and fair elections?

In recent years there were small signs of free elections taking place at village level, e.g. the village of Wukan in March 2012. Following serious protests over corrupt local government officials seizing land, a local village elder, Lin Zuluan, was voted village chief in what were seen by many as genuinely free elections. In some local areas there were experiments with 'deliberative democracy', e.g. in Zeguo where a selected number of residents were asked to vote using the Internet, keypads and other devices about how to spend the town's budget. **However:**

- In 2016, Lin Zuluan was arrested and several villagers were given long prison sentences for protesting against his arrest. Direct elections in which the people cast votes only take place at a village level for Village Committees or local level for a Local People's Congress and candidates have to be approved by the Party.

- ⮕ **Conclusion:** elections may be regular but 'fair' elections are very rare and limited to local level.

A genuine choice between political parties?

Officially there are another eight parties 'allowed' to take part in politics, such as the Jiusan Society, which consists of 'intellectuals' from the fields of science and education. **However:**

- Only the CPC is allowed to stand at a national level.
- The small parties are expected to 'follow the direction' of the CPC.
- Since he became leader, Xi Jinping has increased his own power, including doing away with the two-term limit for the role of president.
- ⮕ **Conclusion:** there is no choice except on a very few occasions at a very local level. Other 'official' parties only exist because the CPC allows them to.

Guaranteed rights such as the right to free speech, protest and protection of the law?

We have already seen that China has what appears to be a very fair and democratic Constitution with guaranteed rights. It is true that in recent years there has been an upsurge in protests, which the Party has 'tolerated'. In some cases, such as the protests against

Japanese control of some islands in the East China Sea, the Party has not only tolerated but encouraged them. **However:**

- According to Amnesty International, China has the largest recorded number of imprisoned journalists and cyber-dissidents in the world.
- China has also been criticised by Amnesty for:
  - persecuting human rights activists
  - detentions without trial
  - the overuse of the death penalty (China executes more people every year than the rest of the world put together)
- Groups, like the spiritual movement Falun Gong, are banned as they could encourage opposition to Communism, which does not allow 'freedom of thought'. Since 1949, an estimated 50 million people have been sent to 're-education camps'. Over 25% of these have been Falun Gong members.
- ➲ **Conclusion:** although there are countries with worse human rights records than China, it is still rated as 'very poor' by international human rights organisations like Amnesty.

A free media not controlled by the government?

It has been easier in recent years for foreign media to report from China, especially in the run-up to the Beijing Olympics in 2008 when China wanted to give a good impression to the rest of the world. **However:**

- Journalists who do not 'toe the Party line' are harassed, arrested and sometimes beaten up.
- The Law on Guarding State Secrets is used to control the media, including social media such as Twitter, Facebook and YouTube. What is actually a 'secret' is never made clear so the law can apply to almost anything.
- Websites that the Party thinks are 'dangerous' are often blocked, especially if there are events that the Party do not want to be reported. Banned sites in recent years have included the BBC's Chinese language website, The New York Times and Wikipedia.
- Certain mobile phone apps, such as WhatsApp, are banned, as the CPC is very concerned about how the Internet played a part in the anti-government protests in the Middle East during the so-called Arab Spring.
- ➲ **Conclusion:** for the above reasons, China is ranked 176 out of 180 countries on the Index of Press Freedom.

Quick Test

1. Describe what has happened recently in the village of Wukan.
2. Is there a 'genuine choice between political parties' in China? Explain your answer.
3. For what reasons have Amnesty International criticised China's record on human rights?
4. Why is the Law on Guarding State Secrets so vague about what a 'secret' actually is?

The importance of China in the world

Is China a superpower?

China's ever growing economic power and its increasing military power mean that it will become an even more important country in the near future. In 2009, for example, China overtook Germany and the USA to become the world's biggest exporter according to the London *Times* newspaper. Some people are even saying that China is the world's next 'superpower'. Evidence to support China being a superpower:

- it has a very large population
- it has a strong economy
- it covers a large land area
- it has a powerful military
- it is increasing the size of its armed forces, and will outspend America by 2040 (source: *Economist* magazine)

However, military experts say that China is not aiming to be a 'global' superpower but is working towards what is called 'anti-access/area denial'. In other words, to become the leading power in the important areas of Asia and the Pacific. China claims this increase in power is a 'peaceful rise' and no threat to peace in the area. In order to increase its economic power, in 2013 China launched what it calls The Belt and Road Initiative, involving spending billions of dollars on infrastructure (roads, railways, bridges, ports, energy supplies etc.) to link China with over 65 countries in Asia, Africa and Europe, to increase trade and open up new export markets for China.

The Chinese economy

As China becomes wealthier, more and more of its people are beginning to enjoy the kind of lifestyle that many people in the West have had for years. China has a rapidly growing middle class. The magazine *Business Insider* estimates that over 500 million people in China will be middle class by 2022. Millions can now afford to buy everything from groceries to luxury goods to cars and foreign holidays. For the West this has many advantages, in particular because many of the goods Chinese consumers are buying are made in the West. The importance of China to the USA, for example, can be seen in the following:

- in 2017 China became the USA's largest trading partner, overtaking Mexico and Canada
- in the ten years from 2008, US sales to China have grown by 86%
- China is the USA's largest lender – around 19% of all of the USA's government bonds were owned by China in 2017

A shopping mall in Shanghai

Impact on the wider world

Because of the rapid growth in Chinese industry and the huge rise predicted for car ownership and electric goods in China, some environmental experts are worried that China's greenhouse gases will continue to rise for quite some time. Since 2007, China has been the world's biggest emitter of greenhouse gases. At the present time, China gets about 70% of its energy from fossil fuels such as coal and oil.

As the Chinese consume more, prices of certain goods will rise, affecting the rest of the world. For example:

- China needs to feed 21% of the world's population with only 9% of the farmland and 6% of the water supply. Food prices across the world are likely to rise as a result
- China is buying up or leasing land in Africa faster than any other country. Some argue however, that because China invests in such things as road systems and irrigation, they also benefit the local communities
- as China eats more and more meat, the price of animal feed will rise
- China's rapidly growing demand for oil will push up oil prices, which in turn will affect the price of most goods

China and Scotland

In December 2011, Chinese pandas Sunshine and Sweetie went on show to the Scottish public at Edinburgh Zoo. At the time, the Scottish Government said that the pandas represented the 'growing friendship' between Scotland and China. In 2018, Scottish Government figures showed that exports of food and drink to China had increased by 150% in ten years. Because of the growing demand for luxury goods in China, Scottish sales of products like whisky and salmon have increased. Scotland also hopes to benefit from the growing demand for renewable energy, such as wind and wave power in China, especially as China has set itself targets to reduce its greenhouse gases. Another benefit to Scotland is the number of Chinese students studying at Scotland's universities. In 2017 there were over 8000 students from China studying in Scotland, nearly twice as many as from any other non-EU country.

EXAM TIP

Be careful when researching information on China as it can be difficult to get an accurate picture of what is happening inside China because of strict government censorship. Try to use more than one source to check for accuracy.

Quick Test

1. Explain why the increase in the number of middle class people in China might benefit countries in the West.
2. Describe some of the problems that this growth might cause across the world.
3. Why is China increasingly important to Scotland?
4. Explain the phrase 'anti-access/area denial' and the Belt and Road Initiative.

Population issues in China

Population control

According to the last population census in 2010, the population of China was 1.3 billion – the largest in the world. The Chinese Government in the 1970s were so concerned that the population of China was growing too fast that they brought in a number of measures to control the number of children people had. People were urged to follow what was called a 'later, longer, fewer' policy, which meant people should wait longer before getting married, leave wide gaps between children and have fewer children.

China has the largest population in the world

From the one-child policy to the three-child policy

Until recently, the main policy to control the growing population was the one-child policy that was introduced in 1979 to try to control the growing population. There were many reported cases of pregnant women who already had a child being taken by local officials to hospital to have the second pregnancy terminated. However, the policy was abandoned in 2015 because of fears of a rapidly falling birth rate, an ageing population and the need for more workers. Now the Chinese government is encouraging women to have more children and some local authorities are even offering incentives such as tax cuts and help with housing. The problem China now has is that many young, educated city-dwelling women are choosing not to have children at all or waiting until they have progressed in their careers to do so.

Effects of population control

There are a number of problems facing the country in the future as a result of population control:

An ageing population

Two things are happening at the same time in China: there are fewer children being born and people are living longer. What will this mean for the future?

- There are not enough children being born to support the ageing population.
- More than a quarter of the Chinese population will be over 65 by 2050.
- By 2050, for every 100 people aged 20–64 there will be 45 people aged over 65 (today it is only 15).
- The 4-2-1 family – children of single-child parents could have to care for two parents and four grandparents.

- Chinese culture stresses the importance of family and respect for older people, and the law in China forces children to look after their parents. However, there are growing numbers of older people whose children cannot or will not look after them.

Gender imbalance

As a result of the strict enforcement of the one-child policy, there are fewer girls being born than boys. Boy children are seen as more desirable than girls because they are more likely to get a better-paid job and so be able to look after their parents when they get older. Although it is against the law to tell pregnant women the gender of their child, many 'unofficial' ultrasound clinics exist. Many women will feel they have to terminate the pregnancy if it is a girl. What will this mean for the future?

Growing gender imbalance

- Although the gap between boy and girl births is falling, it is still high. Since the year 2000, there has been an average of 120 boys being born for every 100 girls.
- By 2020, there will be 24 million more men than women of marriageable age.
- Some women's rights groups are concerned about 'bride trafficking', i.e. buying and selling brides.

Economic effects

- Although the economies of China and India have both grown very rapidly in the last two decades, India has a very young population, which means it will have a very large population of working age for some time to come, whereas China's population is rapidly ageing.
- Although China has started to increase the amount of benefits for older people, such as the National Rural Pension scheme and increased health insurance, it does not provide the same level of health and welfare as governments such as the UK. China will have to increase the amount they spend on these services.
- People may be forced to work longer. At the moment, only about one-fifth of Chinese women living in the cities are still working after 55.
- More people moving to the cities for work means even greater overcrowding.

EXAM TIP

Compare the attitudes of people in China and India to female births. You will see that in both cases a boy is considered more 'valuable' than a girl. This attitude is not uncommon in poorer parts of the world.

Quick Test

1. Describe the recent changes to policies affecting the number of children a woman can have.
2. Explain what the 4-2-1 family means.
3. Why is there a gender imbalance and what problems will this cause in the future?
4. What problems might China face as a result of its ageing population?

Inequality in education

The Chinese school system

Since the introduction of the Revised Compulsory Education Law in 2006, the Chinese education system has provided:

- a minimum of 9 years free and compulsory education for children from ages 6 to 15 years
- 6 years of primary education
- 3 years of junior high school education

Although the education itself is free, parents have to pay fees for materials like books. Teaching in China is very traditional. Children are expected to memorise large amounts of information and then reproduce it in exams. Children and parents, especially in the cities, place a lot of emphasis on getting a good education and, especially, passing the very tough annual exam known as the Gaokao. This exam – the National Higher Education Entrance Examination – takes place over several days. Pupils studying for this exam will take extra classes and do extra homework to make sure they get a place in the university they want.

Success of the Chinese education system

Although it is difficult to make comparisons with other countries because China does not release education statistics for the whole country, there is evidence that the Chinese education system is very effective.

- The last two recent international education comparisons from the Programme for International Students Assessment (PISA) show that parts of China such as Shanghai are out-performing most Western countries in science, reading and maths.

- Each year, Chinese universities produce three times as many graduates in science, technology, engineering and maths as the USA.

- Since the introduction of compulsory free education, China's literacy rate has gone from 67% in 1980 to 96.4% in 2015.

University graduates

EXAM TIP

The CIA World Factbook website has a very useful 'Country Comparisons' section, which allows you to compare one country directly with one or several countries. These pages can be printed off and are a good example of a source you can take in to the assignment write-up.

Inequalities in Chinese education

There are, however, some significant inequalities in Chinese education, especially between urban and rural areas. What are the reasons for this?

A rural school in China

- Rural children drop out of school earlier as they are needed to work on family farms.
- Although the education is free, parents in rural areas often cannot afford the other costs, such as books and school uniforms.
- As most of the jobs in rural areas are farm-related, children often do not see the point in school.
- Because of the Hukou permit system, children of parents who leave their own area in search of work in the cities lose their right to free education and have to pay fees or attend poor-quality private schools.
- Urban children are much more likely to gain college entry than rural children.
- It is difficult to get the best teachers to work in rural areas.

The 13th five-year plan on education

The education in many Chinese schools is based on 'rote learning' – studying and trying to memorise a lot of facts about a subject. This can be very useful in subjects such as science and maths and helps to explain why Chinese students do so well when compared with other countries. However, as the Chinese economy gets bigger, there is a growing need for people who can 'think out of the box' and be creative and come up with new ideas and new products. This is not easy for those who have been simply taught how to 'cram' for exams. As a result, the Chinese Government has introduced changes to the way the education system works as part of the 13th five-year plan on education. Universities and schools are being allowed more freedom to decide how they teach, and there is less emphasis being placed on the results of the Gaokao for getting in to universities.

Quick Test

1. Explain what the Gaokao exam is and why it is so important to many Chinese students.
2. Why do many migrant children not get a good education?
3. What evidence is there that the Chinese education system has had some success in recent years?
4. Why is the Chinese Government concerned about the style of learning in many schools?

Wealth inequality

China's economic divide

By 2032, according to the Centre for Economics and Business Research, China will have overtaken the USA as the world's largest economy. China as a country is becoming much wealthier than it used to be. For example:

- in 2018, there were twice as many new billionaires in China as in the USA
- there is a rapidly growing middle class
- Chinese consumers buy almost one-third of the world's luxury goods
- a World Bank report in 2018 showed that extreme poverty in China fell from 88.3% in 1981, to 1.9% in 2013

However:

- over half of those living in poverty live in ethnic minority areas
- in 2017, according to the US National Bureau of Statistics, there were still over 30 million people living below the poverty line
- there are large and growing wealth gaps between urban and rural areas

The writer Yu Hua described this inequality as 'like walking down a street where on this side are gaudy pleasure palaces and on that side desolate ruins'.

How is the government trying to tackle this inequality?

The Chinese leader Xi Jinping has stated that his War on Poverty will eliminate poverty by 2020 and create a 'moderately prosperous society'. Policies include:

- building millions of low-cost homes
- moving millions of rural poor to cities and towns
- increasing the minimum wage
- increasing benefits for the poorest in society, especially in rural areas

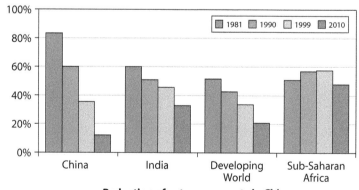

Reduction of extreme poverty in China

Source: World Bank staff estimate

- the new rural cooperative health care system makes it easier for rural poor people to afford health insurance
- the World Bank has stated that since 1981, over 800 million Chinese people have been taken out of poverty

Urban/rural inequality

Although the average income in China has risen rapidly in recent years, the wealth has not been evenly shared out. This is especially true between those who live in the city and those who live in the countryside. It should also be remembered that, despite the rapid growth of China's cities, by 2018, over 40% of the population still lives in the countryside.

Urban and rural income per capita 1978–2012 nominal income, CNY

Urban incomes rising much faster than rural

Note: Per capita disposable income for urban households as defined by NBS; per capita net income for rural households as defined by NBS.

Source: OECD Urban Policy Reviews: China

This chart clearly shows that, although most people in China are better-off than they used to be, some are getting wealthier faster than others. The measure of the gap between the rich and poor in a country is called the Gini coefficient. China now has a higher Gini coefficient than the USA, and is amongst the worst in the world.

Migrant workers

As a result of rural poverty and the attraction of the city, many millions of people are leaving the countryside to look for work in the cities. As a result of this urbanisation, since 1992 almost half of China's 102 cities have grown to a population of over 1 million people each. It is difficult to say exactly how many of these 'migrant' workers there are because many of them will work 'unofficially' but, according to a BBC report in 2018, there are about 300 million migrant workers who work outside their registered area. In China, the Hukou permit system means that each person 'belongs' to a certain area and if they move out of that area they can lose certain rights. For migrant workers it can mean:

* working for low wages
* poor-quality housing – Beijing has banned the renting out of cellars, basements and old air-raid shelters to people without a city Hukou
* loss of state benefits and rights, such as access to education and health care

Although the government is beginning to 'relax' the Hukou regulations to try to create a more urban, better off and skilled population, it is worried that if it relaxes them too much there will be an uncontrolled 'rush' to the cities.

> **EXAM TIP**
>
> A very simple definition of Communism is that everyone in society is given equal shares from the joint efforts of everyone contributing to society: 'from each according to his ability, to each according to his needs'. However, this is very far from the case in China today.

Quick Test

1. Explain the comment made by the writer Yu Hua about life in China today.
2. In what ways has the Chinese Government tried to reduce inequality?
3. What evidence is there that China is making some progress in reducing inequality?
4. Explain the Hukou system and the effect it can have on migrant workers.

Inequality: women in China

'Half the sky'

Over 40 years ago, Mao Zedong who was the 'supreme leader' of China at the time, stated that 'women hold up half the sky'. He said that women had an important part in Chinese society and not just in the home. As we will see, women have made significant progress in China but there are many areas where they have yet to achieve equality.

Women in Chinese politics

As in other areas of life in China, there seems to be a 'glass ceiling' that stops women from reaching the top in politics. Although China today has a higher percentage of women in its Parliament than the USA has in Congress, when it comes to 'real' power, there are far fewer women involved.

- There is only one women out of 25 members of the current Politburo, and there have only ever been five female members.
- There has never been a female member of the real decision-making body, the Standing Committee.
- Since 1949 there have only ever been two female leaders of any of China's Provinces.
- Women make up only 25% of the Chinese Parliament.

Women in business

The rapid growth in the Chinese economy has provided many career opportunities for women that did not exist in the past, and many women have been very successful.

- Eight out of 10 companies in China have women in senior management roles, compared with approximately half in the EU and two-thirds in the USA.
- Ten of the 15 new female billionaires on Forbes's 2018 list of the world's wealthiest people were from China.
- Women now make up 44% of China's workforce.
- As China tries to move away from old 'smoke stack' industries and towards service industries, there will be more opportunities for women who might have been discriminated against in the older industries.

However:
- According to the World Economic Forum's Global Gender Gap Index 2017, China only ranks 100th out of 144 countries listed.
- Women earn on average one-fifth less than men.
- Anti-discrimination laws are not effective as they are often not enforced.

- Although they are entitled to paid maternity leave, many women go back to work early because they are afraid of 'falling behind' their male colleagues.

Reasons for inequality

- There are some very traditional attitudes towards women in Chinese society, which make it difficult for women to achieve equality.
- Even when both partners are working, if they have a child the woman is expected to take care of the home and the child.
- As the population of China gets older as a result of the previous one-child policy, it is the woman in a family who is expected to look after both sets of elderly parents.

Many women in China are carers for elderly relatives

- Employers are reluctant to employ younger women as they feel they will have to take time out to have a family or look after ageing relatives.
- Women who 'put off' having a family in order to focus on their career, risk being labelled as 'leftover women'. Single women over 30, and even in their mid-to-late 20s, can find themselves labelled in this way.

Government action on gender inequality

- Since 2008, the Government has encouraged local governments to employ more women in leadership positions.
- Laws have been introduced in rural areas to protect women's rights on land ownership.
- The Government has insisted that its officials undergo training on gender issues.
- Some quotas have been brought in. For example in cities, at least one of the top four leaders should be female.
- Women are entitled to 3 months paid maternity leave.
- Sexual harassment at work and domestic abuse by husbands has been declared illegal and women have the right to take legal action against those who abuse them.
- In 2005, gender equality was declared a 'national policy'.

Quick Test

1. What evidence is there that women are under-represented in politics in China?
2. Why will the change away from 'smoke stack' industries benefit women?
3. Why does the 'traditional role' of women in Chinese society make it more difficult for women to follow their career than men?
4. What has the Chinese Government done in recent years to try to improve female equality?

Tackling inequality in China

The 13th Five-Year Plan

Every five years, the government of China produces a five-year plan. These set out what the government intends to do over the course of the next five years. The 13th Five-Year Plan will run from 2016 to 2020, and there are a number of targets aimed at reducing inequality:

- reducing inequality is to be as important as improving the economy
- industries such as tourism and e-commerce encouraged in rural areas
- reducing the gap between living standards in urban and rural areas
- a Health Action Plan aiming at providing health care for all by 2020
- making sure all children get a basic education and skills training to improve chances of a job
- elderly and people with disabilities to receive increased benefits paid by the government
- millions of low-cost houses to be built

China's minimum wage

In 1994 the Chinese Government passed the Labour Law, which introduced a minimum wage:

- it should be enough to guarantee that workers can meet their everyday needs
- most cities set a minimum wage that employers must pay their workers
- the richer areas can afford to pay a higher level than the poorer areas; some states set high minimum wage, e.g. Shanghai has the highest minimum wage, worth the equivalent of US$322.58 per month
- many workers complain that price rises 'eat up' the increase in wages
- many employers just take more money off the workers' wages to pay for the rise

Health care

According to the *British Medical Journal* in 2017, approximately 95% of the Chinese population were provided with a basic level of health insurance and people were having to pay much less from their own money for health care. Chinese leader Xi Jinping has promised that the Healthy China Plan 2030 will provide essential health services for every Chinese citizen by 2030. Life expectancy in China has improved significantly in recent years. In 2016, the World Health Organization stated that healthy life expectancy in China overtook the USA. However, there is evidence of continuing inequality in health care, especially between urban and rural areas, for example:

- the insurance provided does not 'cover' long or expensive treatments
- drug shortages affect the rural areas much more than the city areas

- there are far fewer nurses, doctors and hospital beds per head in rural areas than in urban areas
- death rates in rural areas are 30% higher than in city areas

Housing

In the past, the Hukou system that registers each person as 'belonging' to a specific place prevented migrant workers from legally moving to the cities and so they did not qualify for certain benefits, access to local schools, government housing etc. However, as the government is now trying to encourage people to move to the cities to modernise the economy, the Hukou system is being 'relaxed'. The 13th Five-Year Plan has promised to make it easier for migrant workers to qualify for affordable housing as well as continuing to build millions of affordable houses each year. These measures, however, are often criticised:

- many of the cities that are attractive to migrants such as Beijing are seen as 'full' and local authorities are stopping migrant workers from settling
- the number of affordable houses being built is much less than is needed
- officials in some of the largest cities have demolished what they call 'illegal structures', mostly housing poorer people and migrant workers

Job creation

In July 2012, former Chinese Premier Wen Jiabao stated: 'The task of promoting full employment will be very heavy and we must make greater efforts to achieve it.'

As part of the 13th Five-Year Plan, the Chinese Government has said it will create 50 million jobs by 2020. The 'Internet Plus Agriculture' policy aims not only to create more jobs in farming, but also to encourage newer, modern industries in rural areas. Government grants and loans will be targeted at employers and new businesses who take on a lot of workers. Although these and previous policies had brought unemployment in 2017 down to its lowest level since 2001, there are still many problems including changing from old 'smoke stack' industries to more modern skills-based jobs and getting workers to go to the areas of the country where they are needed most.

Quick Test

1. In what ways is the 13th Five-Year Plan aimed at reducing inequality?
2. Explain how the minimum wage works and why some workers think it is not enough.
3. How is the Chinese government tackling inequality in two of the following?
    (a) health
    (b) housing
    (c) employment

Government of India: 1

India's federal government

India is a democracy – in fact it is the world's largest democracy. In the 2014 general election over 537 million people voted, making it the largest democratic vote in the world ever. India has a federal government, which means that there is a central government for the whole country – called the Union Government – and state governments for each of the 29 states shown below.

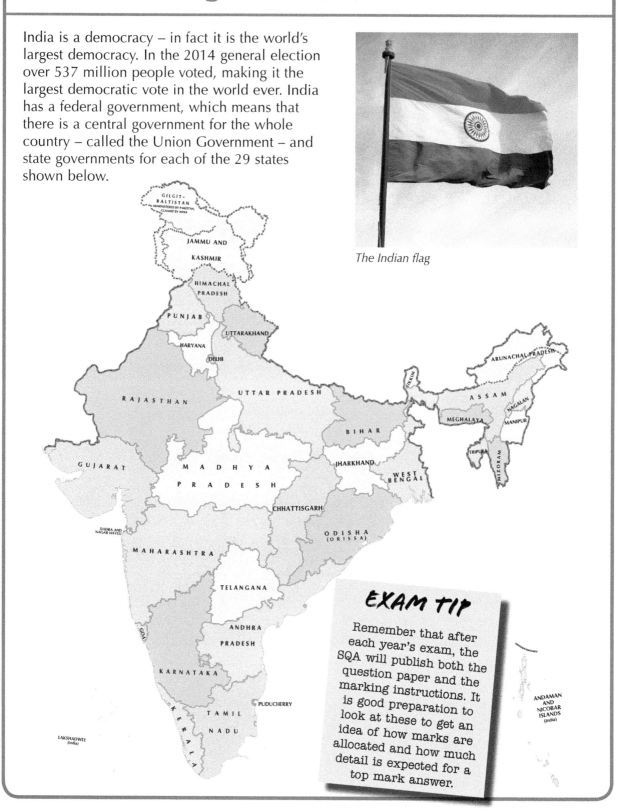

The Indian flag

EXAM TIP

Remember that after each year's exam, the SQA will publish both the question paper and the marking instructions. It is good preparation to look at these to get an idea of how marks are allocated and how much detail is expected for a top mark answer.

Branches of the government

The Government of India, like many democracies, divides the powers of government among different 'branches'. Here is how it works in India:

Power of government	Definition	Branches of the Indian Government
Legislative power	The power to make new laws or change existing ones.	Parliament & President
Executive power	To make decisions in the day-to-day running of the country.	The Prime Minister and the Council of Minsters
Judicial power	To make sure the laws are upheld and enforced.	The Supreme Court

The Indian Parliament

The Indian Parliament is 'bi-cameral' ('two chambers'), which means that there are two houses, in the same way that the UK Parliament has the House of Commons and the House of Lords. In India they are known as the House of the People (Lok Sabha), which is the lower house, and the Council of States (Rajya Sabha), which is the upper house.

What powers does the Indian Parliament have?

• It passes laws on the matters for which it has constitutional responsibility.

• It approves (and can remove) members of the Council of Ministers.

• It amends the Constitution.

• It approves central government's finances.

• It can also change the boundaries of the state and union territories in India.

Quick Test

1. Explain what is meant by a 'federal government' and describe how this works in India.

2. In your own words, describe the role of each of the branches of the Indian Government.

3. Describe the similarities between the Indian and UK governments.

Government of India: 2

Branches of government

The legislative, executive and judicial powers of the Indian Government are shared by the different branches:

- The Parliament
- The President
- The Prime Minister and the Council of Ministers
- The Supreme Court

They operate in a system of 'checks and balances', which means that each branch can amend or veto the acts of another so that no one branch can have too much power.

On page 85 we learned about the Parliament, and here we will look at the other branches.

EXAM TIP

You can gain up to 4 marks in an 'explain' type answer for **each** detailed explanation supported by accurate and relevant examples. Avoid list type answers!

The Prime Minister and the Council of Ministers

Most of the real power to make decisions in India lies with the Prime Minister and the Council of Ministers. Again, there are similarities with the UK, as the Indian Prime Minster will be the leader of the biggest party (or coalition) in the Lok Sabha (House of the People). The Indian Prime Minister has a great deal of power as this diagram shows:

Indian Prime Minister, Narendra Modi

Decides which members of the Council of Minsters gets which job in government

Prime Minister

Leads the Council of Ministers meetings and decides what is discussed

Chief adviser to the President

Hires and fires members of the Council of Ministers

The Supreme Court

The Supreme Court is the highest court in India. It is made up of a Chief Justice and 25 other judges. Although the President appoints Supreme Court judges when a vacancy occurs, they are appointed 'on the advice' of the Prime Minister. The Supreme Court in India has a number of powers and functions, for example:

- it is the highest court of appeal; when a person or a body is not satisfied with the decision of a lower court, they can appeal to a higher court, and the Supreme Court is the final court of appeal
- ruling on disputes between states or between the central government and states
- deciding whether an action or a decision or a law 'fits in' with India's Constitution (the rules about how the country is run); if it does not consider something to be constitutional, it can stop it or amend it
- making decisions that must be followed by all lower courts

The President

According to the Constitution of India, the President would appear to be a very powerful person with responsibility for a range of matters including:

- giving final approval to all new laws
- 'dissolving' Parliament (i.e. deciding when a parliamentary session should end and an election be held)
- choosing the Prime Minister and the Council of Ministers
- appointing the Chief Justice and other judges of the Supreme Court

However, as the President can only do these things on the 'advice' of the Prime Minister and the Council of Ministers, the President, like the Monarch in the UK, does not have the opportunity to exercise any real power, and is largely a ceremonial position.

Quick Test

1. Explain what is meant by 'checks and balances'.
2. Apart from the President, which branch of the Indian Government do you think is the most powerful? Give reasons for your answer.
3. 'The role of President in India carries no real power.' What evidence is there to support this statement?

How democratic is India?

The key features of a democracy

Before we can say whether or not India (or any country) is a democracy we need to be clear about what the key features of a democracy are so that we have something to 'measure against'.

- Guaranteed rights such as the right to vote and freedom of speech.
- Regular and fair elections.
- A genuine choice between political parties.
- A free media not controlled by the government.

Is India democratic?

Like many questions in Modern Studies, the answer to this one is 'to some extent'. India does have the key features of a democracy but there have been, and still are, areas where what actually takes place can be described as less than 'democratic'.

EXAM TIP

For whichever country or countries you study, make sure you are able to describe the ways in which they are able to exert influence and power in world affairs.

Guaranteed rights

India has one of the longest written constitutions in the world, which guarantees the people of India the following rights (among others):

- equality before the law
- freedom of speech, expression and peaceful assembly (i.e. gathering and meeting with others)
- freedom to practice religion
- freedom from exploitation
- cultural and educational rights
- the right to life

However, the caste system, the position of women and the great differences between the rich and poor in India mean that, for many, they do not enjoy all of the rights outlined above.

Regular and fair elections

India has elections for many posts at state, territory and national level. The elections for the Indian Parliament take place every 5 years and the states each hold regular elections for their Assemblies. In fact, because of the size of India and the number of separate states, there are elections somewhere in the country at least every 6 months. There are concerns, however, about the levels of corruption. A survey in 2017 by Transparency International, which monitors corruption across the world, stated that India has the highest bribery rate among the 16 Asia Pacific countries. In the same year, *The Economist* magazine stated '34% of the members of parliament (MPs) in the Lok Sabha (lower house) have criminal charges filed against them; and the figure is rising'.

A genuine choice between political parties

India is a multi-party democracy. After the 2014 election there were 40 different parties with MPs in the Lok Sabha. They ranged from the Bharatiya Janata Party (BJP) with 272 seats to the Jan Adhikar Party with one seat. Although the Indian National Congress Party (INC) has held power most often since independence, there have been other parties and coalitions that have governed India in the past.

A free media not controlled by the government

Why is a free media important in a democracy?

An Indian man reads one of the 70,000 newspapers available in India

- It keeps the people informed about what is happening in the country so they can make 'informed' choices when voting.
- It will act as a 'watchdog' by publicising government actions.
- It allows the people to express their views inbetween elections.

In recent years, India has seen an 'explosion' in the number of newspapers and news channels, as well as a huge growth in the numbers of people with access to the Internet and social media such as Twitter and Facebook. It is estimated that there are around 70,000 newspapers and 80 separate news channels available in India, expressing many different points of view, often against the government. As well as keeping the Indian people informed about what is happening, they have played a large part in bringing to light many of the corruption scandals. However, the following points should also be noted about the media in India:

- in the World Press Freedom Index in 2107, India only ranked 136 out of 180 countries
- a study by the Centre for the Study of Developing Societies showed that over 75% of all decision-makers in TV and the press were from the upper castes
- in 2017, Reporters Without Borders reported that 17 Indian journalists had been killed
- Amnesty International published a report in 2017 on press freedom in India in which it stated, 'Repressive laws were used to stifle freedom of expression, and journalists and press freedom came under increasing attack'.

Quick Test

1. Explain how you would decide how democratic a country is.
2. Do all Indians receive the rights that they are supposed to be 'guaranteed' by the Constitution? Give evidence for your answer.
3. Explain why a free media is important in a democracy.
4. Why is India ranked so low in the World Press Freedom Index?

India's importance in the world

Why should we study India?

Because of its size, its position, the fact that it has nuclear weapons and its growing importance to the world's economy, India is becoming an increasingly important world power.

The Indian economy
- India is a member of the group known as the G20, which consists of the 19 strongest economies in the world plus the European Union.
- In 2018, India became the seventh biggest economy in the world. The UK, by comparison, was fifth.
- In 2018, the World Bank ranked India as the third fastest growing economy.
- India has a skilled and educated workforce, which makes it attractive to foreign investors.

India and Scotland
The Scottish Government recognises the importance of India to Scotland in its 2010 'India Plan', which focuses on four key areas – tourism, education and science, trade and investment, and cultural links. Scotland hopes to benefit from the growing demand for 'luxury' items like whisky. In 2017, India was the third biggest buyer of Scottish whisky. In an attempt to attract more students from India, in 2018, scholarships worth £1 million were made available to outstanding students from India to study in Scotland.

India and the UK
The 2017 report of the Congress of Indian Industry (CII) showed how important India is to the UK economy, with approximately 800 Indian companies operating in the UK and investing over £4 billion in 2016 alone. Companies from the technology, telecoms, pharmaceuticals and chemicals sectors were the most prominent and fastest growing in the UK. In total, Indian companies employed approximately 110,000 workers. When this book was written, the UK was in the process of leaving the European Union and although trade with India is small compared with trade with the European Union, India is seen as an important future trade partner if the UK leaves the EU, especially as the Indian middle class is increasing rapidly and, as in China, are buying more of the sort of goods made in the UK. The UK is also home to many Indian origin super-rich people, with the Times Rich List of 2018 showing that the Hiduja brothers were the second richest people in the UK and that the top 1000 super rich contained 40 people of Indian origin.

UK and India leaders discuss trade deals

Why is India becoming increasingly important in the world?

- India is the largest and most powerful country in the area around the Indian Ocean. For the most part, India is a 'stable' democracy. This is important in an area that has seen many conflicts in the past.
- It is important that the area around the Indian Ocean remains peaceful because:
  - around 40% of offshore oil production takes place there
  - 65% of the world's total oil supply and 35% of its gas supply comes from countries around the Indian Ocean
  - nearly half of all the world's trade by sea passes through the area

> **EXAM TIP**
>
> If answering a question about the influence of a country such as India, as well as discussing political, military and economic influences, you can also include how Indian culture – food, music, art etc. – has influenced many countries around the world.

- India is a nuclear power. The Arms Control Association estimated in 2018 that India has around 135 nuclear weapons. Its close neighbour, Pakistan, also has nuclear weapons. In the past, India and Pakistan have come into conflict on several occasions, although, apart from tension over the disputed areas of Kashmir, relations between the two countries have been more peaceful in recent years.

An Indian nuclear weapon on display at a Republic Day Parade

- As China increases its influence in Southeast Asia, the West sees India as becoming more important in countering this influence. The USA sees India as part of 'the Quad' of democracies worried about the rise of China, along with Japan, the USA and Australia. India on the other hand does more trade with China than the USA and is trying to improve relations with China.

Quick Test

1. Briefly explain why we should study India.
2. What evidence is there that India's economy is becoming more and more important to the word?
3. Why is the Scottish Government trying to encourage stronger links with India?
4. Explain the purpose of the so-called 'Quad' of democracies.

Population issues in India

Key population facts

With its 1.3 billion people, India is second in size only to China; however, at the present rate of population growth, India will overtake China by 2025 to become the world's most populated state. The population of India has more than tripled in the last 60 years.

Key fact	India	UK
Current population	1.3 billion	66.6 million
Birth rate per 1000 people	31	12
Major languages	Hindi, English and 16 other official languages	English, regional languages (Gaelic, Welsh)
Major religions	Hindu (80.5%), Muslim (13.4), Christian (2.3%), Sikh (1.9%)	Christian (71.6%) Muslim, (2.7%), Hindu (1%), Unspecified or none (23.1%)
Median age	26.5 years	40.2 years
Life expectancy	69.9 years	80.17 years
Population growth rate	1.1% per year	0.59% per year
Infant deaths per 100 live births	37	4.56
Percentage living in urban areas	33.5%	83%
Urbanisation rate per year*	2.4%	0.7%
Sex ratio	1.8 males to every female	0.99 males to every female
Largest city	Mumbai 18.4 million	London 8.615 million

*urbanisation = moving to towns and cities

(Source: *The CIA World Fact Book*)

What then can we take from this information about the population of India?
* India's population is young and rapidly growing.
* It is ethnically and culturally mixed.
* People are moving to the cities but India is still a mostly rural society.
* There are fewer girls than boys.
* It has some of the largest cities in the world.

Problems caused by a growing population

- Growing pressure on natural resources to meet the needs of its expanding population.
- The charity Water Aid states that there are vast numbers of people living without sanitation or water, and that only 15% of the rural population have access to a toilet.
- Activities such as logging and mining are causing damage to the environment.
- More people, more cars, more electrical goods and more factories means more pollution.
- India needs to spend more and more on imports from other countries.
- Rapidly growing demands for education, housing, health care and jobs.

Why is the population of India growing?

Although the population of India continues to grow, fertility rates (i.e. the number of children born per woman) have been declining. Since the 1950s there have been various government attempts to try to slow down the rate of population growth. Some of these measures were very unpopular. In the 1970s the Indian Government under Indira Gandhi was accused of trying to introduce compulsory sterilisation for certain groups of people such as men who had already had two children. This was very controversial and unpopular. Since then, family planning has been a very sensitive issue and one that many politicians are unwilling to tackle. Why do some people have more children than others?

- In rural areas, children can work on farms and in urban areas they can earn money for the family.
- Lack of education – the more educated a person is, the more likely they are to use family planning, know how to access health care and keep children healthy.
- In rural areas, family planning advice may not be easy to access.
- Children are needed to look after parents when the parents can no longer work, because many poor people will not have a pension or savings etc.
- The high child death rate in some areas means people have more children.

However, not all groups in Indian society have large families. The better-off and the better-educated have smaller than average families and people in the south of India, which is more prosperous, have fewer children.

Quick Test

1. Use six keywords to summarise the main features of the population of India.
2. Describe the problems that India faces as a result of the growing population.
3. Why do some people have more children than others?

Population issues in India: the move to the cities

Urbanisation

Ever since the Industrial Revolution, more and more people around the world have left the countryside and moved to the towns and cities. This migration is known as urbanisation. Today, urbanisation is taking place much faster in the less economically developed countries (LEDCs) than in the more economically developed countries (MEDCs). In recent years, India has seen one of the fastest rates of urbanisation in the world.

The story of Ujjwal gives some idea of why so many people are moving to India's cities.

'Ujjwal is a 22-year-old labourer sitting outside a makeshift tent in a posh part of New Delhi. By day he works on repaving the road. By night he sleeps on the pavement. Like millions of Indians, he has migrated to the big city to find work and earn money. It is the only way he can gain any benefit from the mainly-urban economic boom which has swept through this country. "There are so many more opportunities available here than there are at home," he says. "You have to work hard and the hours are long. But I don't want to go back to my village in Bengal. I want to stay here in Delhi".'

A crowded street in Old Delhi

(Source: BBC News at bbc.co.uk/news)

Distress migration

As well as people being *drawn* to cities because of the opportunities, many are *forced* to leave the countryside. It is increasingly difficult to make a living in rural areas in India. According to government figures, in an article in the *Times of India* in 2017, there have been 12,000 suicides in agricultural areas every year since 2013. Many farmers were in a great deal of debt as they tried to change from food farming to growing cash crops, which require expensive seeds and chemicals. Growing cash crops also requires more water, which is in short supply in many parts of rural India. This sort of migration from the countryside to the city has been called 'distress migration'.

Other reasons for urbanisation

- There are more jobs available in the towns and cities – including 'unofficial' jobs.
- Better access to services such as water, electricity, schools and hospitals.
- Cultural attractions such as cinemas, theatres, restaurants etc.
- The Indian Government's 'modernisation' policies (five-year plans) have focused on manufacturing and service jobs, which are based in towns and cities.

Problems caused by urbanisation

Most of India's megacities like Mumbai and Dehli have very modern buildings, shopping complexes and luxurious hotels, much like many European cities. They also have large numbers of prosperous people; in fact, India had the fastest growing number of millionaires in the world in 2018. However, alongside this wealth, there are many millions living in poverty and in slum conditions. Many of India's cities are simply not coping with the increase in their population; some of the problems include:

A slum in Mumbai

- over half of India's population has no access to adequate toilets
- growing demand for water in cities means that 21 of India's largest cities could run out of groundwater supplies by 2020 according to an Indian Government report in 2018
- the demand for water from the cities is leaving less water for rural areas
- the population living in slums has doubled in the last 20 years
- almost half of the people in India's second largest city, Delhi, live in slums
- these problems are slowing down the economic development of the megacities like Mumbai and Dehli

Quick Test

1. Explain what is meant by 'urbanisation'.
2. Why are many people in rural areas in India finding it difficult to meet their needs?
3. Apart from rural poverty, what other reasons are given for 'urbanisation'?
4. Describe the types of problems this urbanisation is causing in India.

Inequality: education in India

The right to education

'The child is entitled to receive education, which shall be free and compulsory, at least in the elementary stages.'

The United Nations Declaration of the Rights of the Child

'The World cannot reach its goal of primary education for all children by 2015 without India.'

UNICEF report

In India, education is a fundamental right of every Indian child according to the Constitution. However, not all children in India have full access to education, with many facing inequality.

International comparisons

A recent OECD report compared Indian education with 'similar' countries, such as Brazil, Russia and China, and found that India had:

- a far lower percentage of its young people enrolled in higher education
- poorer employability for Indian graduates
- lower standards of reading and writing
- school attendance numbers on a day-to-day basis that are affected by the poor health of children
- India has no universities in the list of the top 100 in the world

EXAM TIP

You can 'follow' organisations such as UNICEF, who use social media to get their message across. This can be really useful for up-to-date examples – and they do most of the work for you!

What are the reasons for this?

- **Differences between states** – some states in India are better-off than others and can provide better education. The states in the south and west are more prosperous than those in the north and east and this affects the quality of education. For example, there is a 40% gap between literacy in the poor state of Bihar compared with the wealthier state of Kerala. It is estimated that the two-thirds of children in the whole of India who do not attend school live in just five of the poorest states in India.

- **Gender and caste** – in India women and girls and people from lower castes face inequality in many areas of life, and that includes education. According to UNICEF, girls in India are less likely to attend schools, especially in rural areas, and are less likely to be able to read and write. Dalit children also face discrimination; a study by the University of Dublin in 2011 found that compared to the Brahmin or high caste groups, Dalit children did much worse in reading, writing and arithmetic. In the state of Bihar, for example, only 19% of the Dalit population can read and write.

- **Wealth** – most schools and universities in India are provided by the government; however, in recent years there has been a significant increase in the number of children of the wealthy middle classes, especially in the cities, attending expensive private schools. One of the reasons for this is that most teach in English, which many see as being preferable to the regional languages taught in most government schools. Many poorer families prefer to send their children to private school even if they have to make sacrifices to pay the fees as the quality of education in state schools is often very poor. However, for the very poor, paying any fees at all is simply not possible, so state schools tend to have higher numbers of the very poor.

Attempts to reduce inequality

There have been many attempts by both the national government and the governments of the various states to try to reduce inequality in education, as outlined in the table below

Right of Children to Free and Compulsory Education (RTE) Act 2009	• Free compulsory education for all children aged 6 to 14. • 25% of places in private schools are reserved for poor children. • Neighbourhood school-building programmes. • Stricter rules on qualifications for teachers.
Rashtriya Madhyamik Shiksha Abhiyan (RMSA)	• Aims to expand and improve secondary education. • Aims to eventually provide secondary education for all. • Ensures that there will be a secondary school within 5 km for all children.
Anganwadi systems	• Schemes which brought children from particularly poor households into schools. • Help is also given with food and health needs to allow the children to attend schools.
The National Programme for Education of Girls at Elementary Level (NPEGEL)	• To improve education for all girls and to encourage the 'hardest to reach' girls in poor and rural areas to attend school.

How effective have these policies been? According to a recent World Bank report:

- since 2001, the RMSA programme brought over 20 million children into primary education
- 99% of rural children live within 1 km of a school
- 24 out of India's 29 states have near total primary school enrollment
- a higher percentage of girls are now enrolled in school than ever before
- across India, almost 95% of children attend primary school

Quick Test

1. What evidence is there that India is not doing as well in education as it should?
2. Describe the main reasons for inequality in education.
3. What evidence is there that policies to improve education are having some success?

Inequality: the caste system

Caste discrimination

India's caste system divides the population in to certain groups or 'castes'. A person born into a caste remains within it for their whole life.

However, there is another group outside of the caste system that is made up of those called the 'untouchables' or Dalits. This group tend to do the jobs that are traditionally seen as 'unclean', such as working with leather, handling meat, cleaning streets and toilets and preparing the dead for burial. Their very presence, even their shadow, is regarded by some higher caste members as 'polluting'. People classed as 'untouchable' face many restrictions in their daily life. They are often prevented from the following:

- eating with those from higher castes
- marrying those from higher castes
- sitting in the same areas as higher castes
- using the same utensils as higher castes in restaurants
- entering into village temples
- wearing sandals or holding umbrellas in front of those from higher caste
- entering higher caste homes
- riding a bicycle inside their village
- sitting beside higher caste children in schools

Despite the Indian Government banning discrimination on the grounds of caste, and the UN declaring caste discrimination a human rights abuse, it still affects large numbers of people. 16% of the Indian population are in the lowest caste group and this affects their life chances. For example, many Dalits in some parts of India suffer from:

- lower wages
- high drop-out rates from education – after the age of 15, only 60% of Dalits are still in school
- illiteracy – literacy among Dalits is 66% compared to 73% in the rest of the population
- lack of land ownership, as this is not allowed in many areas
- higher levels of poverty and malnutrition

EXAM TIP

There are many life stories of people affected by these issues on YouTube. It is always useful to hear information first-hand from the people affected by it. A simple search for 'Dalits in India' will find many documentaries on the subject.

Tackling caste discrimination

As far back as 1955 the Indian Government passed the Untouchability Offences Act, which was supposed to outlaw caste discrimination. However, it had little effect and The Prevention of Atrocities Act 1989 was needed. The Indian Government has come under growing pressure from organisations like the UN, The National Campaign on Dalit Human Rights and the Dalit Freedom Network to deal with caste discrimination. In some Indian states such as Utter Pradesh, Dalit political parties are becoming more powerful. In order to lessen the impact of caste, the Indian Government has introduced several measures including:

- declaring caste discriminations illegal and against the Constitution
- introducing 'affirmative action' policies, which include making sure that a certain amount – or quota – of government jobs, university places and places in school are kept aside for Dalits
- giving small government loans in instalments to Dalit businesses
- ensuring a percentage of elected positions are 'reserved' for Dalits

Contrasting lifestyles among Dalits

Although some Dalits, such as Kalpana Saroj, have been very successful, for many more Dalits their lives are similar to that of Veerasamy.

Kalpana Saroj	Veerasamy
• Married at age 12. • Dropped out of school at 14. • Became a seamstress to make a living after leaving her violent husband and his family. • Takes over struggling metal tubes company and makes it a success. • Becomes chief executive of Kamani Tubes, a company worth over $100 million.	• Lives in a small village in southern India where all the villagers are 'outcasts'. • Belongs to the lowest group within the Dalits. • Takes in the washing of the 19 families in the village to make a living. • His wife and family help him to do the washing. • The only payment he gets is the leftovers from other people's meals.

Quick Test

1. Briefly describe the caste system in India.
2. How does the caste system affect the lives of people in the lower castes, such as the Dalits?
3. In what ways has the Government of India tried to reduce the impact of the caste system?

Inequality: women and girls

Successful Indian women

There are women in India who have achieved positions of power and influence, including women such as Sonia Gandhi, who headed one of India's biggest political parties, the Indian National Congress Party and Sushma Swaraj, a Supreme Court lawyer and the leader of the Bharatiya Janata Party (BJP). In fact, one of the most powerful figures in the history of modern India was Indira Gandhi, India's first female Prime Minister. There are also women in very powerful positions in business, including Chanda Kochhar who is currently the CEO of ICICI Bank – India's second largest bank. Women in India today are doctors, lawyers, police officers and politicians. However, for many women in India, the situation is very different. Despite the success of women like those above, only 11% of India's Members of Parliament are female. In fact, according to Gulshum Rehman of Save the Children: 'In India, women and girls continue to be sold as chattels, married off as young as 10, burned alive as a result of dowry-related disputes and young girls are exploited and abused as domestic slave labour'.

Women and girls in India

- Five women die every hour in childbirth in India.
- 75% of women work on the land, but only 13% of the land is owned by women.
- Less than two-thirds of women in rural areas are literate.
- The National Crime Record Bureau estimates that there are 21 'dowry deaths' every day.
- The percentage of women working in India is the lowest in the G20.
- India has the highest number of child brides in the world.

In 2018, the Thomson Reuters Foundation named India as the worst place to be a woman out of all the G20 countries. There are many reasons for this gender inequality, including the following:

- There is a preference for male children. The 2011 census of India showed 914 female live births for every 1000 live male births. (Figures from the previous census show that this gap is getting bigger.) Although they are illegal, sex-selective abortions have been blamed for some of this gap. Families often put pressure on mothers to have child after child until a boy is born.

- The 'traditional' view in some areas (especially the north), is that women and girls are 'inferior' and must be restricted to homemaking and child rearing.

- Many see girls as a burden because of dowries that families feel they have to pay in order to get a 'good' husband.

- Women in lower castes face even greater prejudice and discrimination.

- Adolescent marriage: India has one of the highest rates of adolescent marriage in the world. Adolescent mothers in most cases do not complete their education.

Reducing gender inequality in India

In recent years the state and national governments of India have introduced many measures to try to tackle gender inequality.

Action	Intentions
Equal rights guaranteed by the Constitution	• To prevent discrimination on the grounds of gender, race, caste etc. • To uphold the principle of equality for all before the law. • To guarantee equal opportunity in matters relating to employment.
2009 and 2010 changes to the Constitution	• Increased the number of places set aside for women in the village councils to 50%. • Increased the number of the seats in the national and state parliaments for women.
Set up The National Commission for Women (NCW) in 1992	• To safeguard the interests of women in India. • To investigate abuses. • To recommend actions, including new laws.
The Prohibition of Child Marriage Act 2006	• Outlawed marriages for females under 18 and males under 21.
Sexual Harassment of Women in the Workplace Act 2013	• To protect women from sexual harassment in the workplace.
Married Women's Property Act 1974, and the Hindu Succession Act 1956	• Strengthened women's rights to their own property and to inherit property and land.

However, although these measure and others are improving the position of women in India today, they are not always strictly enforced, especially in the rural areas where traditional attitudes are still very strong.

Quick Test

1. What evidence is there that it is possible for at least some women in India to become successful?

2. Explain why India has been ranked as the worst place in the G20 to be a female.

3. What attempts have been made by the Indian Government to tackle gender inequality?

The Government of the USA: 1

Representative democracy

Like India and the UK, the USA is a democracy – or to be more accurate, a representative democracy. In other words, the people choose (usually by voting) the people they want to represent them.

In the USA, there are many elections for political positions at various levels, from city to state to federal. The USA is a federal system, which means that each of the 50 states has its own government or assembly, with responsibility for certain things within that state, while the federal government is responsible for certain things across the whole country.

Some of these powers are shown in the table below.

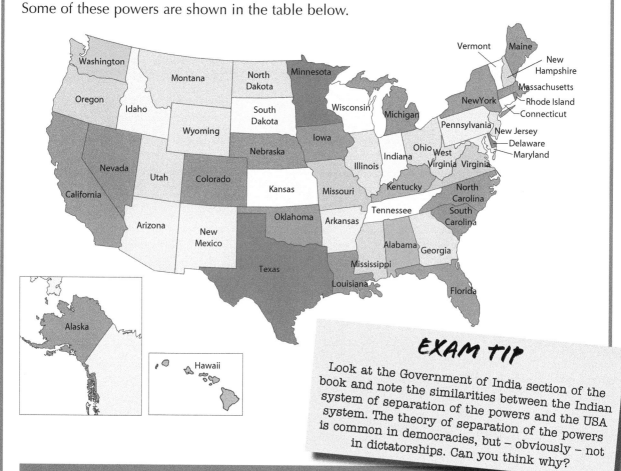

EXAM TIP

Look at the Government of India section of the book and note the similarities between the Indian system of separation of the powers and the USA system. The theory of separation of the powers is common in democracies, but – obviously – not in dictatorships. Can you think why?

Federal powers	State powers
Coin money (i.e. control the money in circulation)	Manage public health and safety
Declare war	Oversee trade within the state
Conduct foreign relations	Education
Oversee foreign and interstate trade	Whether or not to apply the death penalty

The federal government

When the original writers of the United States Constitution sat down to write the 'rules' of how the USA should be governed, they were determined that no one person or part of the government should have too much power. So, as with the Indian Constitution, the Constitution of the USA separates the powers of government among three different branches.

Power of government	Meaning	Branches of the US Government
Legislative power	The power to make new laws or change existing ones	Congress
Executive power	To make decisions in the day-to-day running of the country	The President
Judicial power	To make sure the laws are upheld and enforced	The Supreme Court

Checks and balances

In order to ensure that the powers remained 'separate', a system of checks and balances was built in.

President appoints Supreme Court Judges.

President can 'veto' (reject) a law passed by Congress.

President can suggest new laws.

Congress can pass new laws.

Senate has to approve choice.

Congress can overturn a veto by a 2–3 vote.

Only Congress can pass new laws.

The Supreme Court can reject them if they are 'unconstitutional'.

Quick Test

1. Explain what is meant by 'Separation of the powers' and 'Checks and balances'. Give examples to illustrate your answers.

2. Describe the similarities between the Indian and the US political systems mentioned here.

The Government of the USA: 2

The US Congress

Just as in India where there are two 'houses' in Parliament, the same is true of the United States. The legislative or law-making part of the federal government is called 'Congress'. Congress is divided into two parts – the House of Representatives and the Senate. The main job of Congress is to prepare, debate and pass bills, which are then sent to the President for approval.

House of Representatives

Responsible for all bills to do with revenue or tax raising.

Can impeach officials, including the President, for wrongdoing.

The Senate

Approves many government appointments.

Approves all treaties signed by the President.

Congress meets in the Capitol building in Washington D.C.

Why two houses?

When the Founding Fathers were writing the Constitution, smaller states were worried that they would not be very powerful compared to so their larger neighbours. To make sure that each state had a 'voice', they are each represented in the Senate by two Senators, regardless of the size of the state. That is why there are 100 Senators – two for each of the 50 states. However, in order to ensure that states with larger populations are fairly represented, each state elects a number of 'Representatives' according to the size of their population. For example, California has 53 seats in the House of Representatives while seven states, such as Wyoming and North Dakota, have only one.

The Supreme Court

The judicial power of the political system of the USA is carried out by the courts. The Supreme Court is the highest court in the USA. It consists of nine Supreme Court judges appointed by the President and approved by the Senate. They are appointed for life and cannot be removed unless they are 'impeached'. This is intended to make sure they remain 'independent'.

The role of the Supreme Court includes:

- hearing cases that have made their way through lower courts and have been 'appealed'; the Supreme Court's decisions are final
- 'protecting' the Constitution – i.e. making sure that any laws passed or decisions taken do not go against the Constitution

Some of the decisions of the Supreme Court have had a very big impact on the lives of millions of American citizens, for example:

- Brown v. Board of Education ruled that segregating schools on the basis of race was unconstitutional and had 'no place in public education'. This forced many states to end the practice of providing separate schools for Blacks and Whites.
- Gideon v. Wainwright ruled that, 'anyone charged with a serious criminal offence has the right to an attorney and the state must provide one if they are unable to afford legal counsel'.

The President

The President of the United States is responsible for the executive function of government. Although the system of Checks and Balances and the Separation of the Powers puts limits on the power of the President, he (there has never been a female President) is a very powerful figure.

Makes sure laws passed by Congress are carried out

Appoints Supreme Court Judges when a vacancy occurs

Approves, and can veto new laws from Congress

Commander-in-Chief of the armed forces

Can propose new laws to Congress

EXAM TIP

Supreme Court judges are nominated by the President who will usually suggest people who hold similar views to his political party. When this book was written there were eight judges, four each having been nominated by Democratic Presidents and Republican Presidents. There was one vacancy. Find out who has filled the vacancy, as their views could 'tip the balance' of overall opinion in the Supreme Court.

Quick Test

1. Explain why the Supreme Court can have a big impact on the lives of many Americans.
2. Why might the appointment of the next Supreme Court judge 'tip the balance' of opinion in the Court?
3. What evidence is there that the President plays a part in each of the powers of government?

How democratic is the USA?

The features of a democracy

We have already seen that there are certain 'key features' of a democracy that can be used to measure whether or not a country is a democracy. So, how democratic is the USA?

Guaranteed rights

The rights of the citizens of the USA are clearly set out in a number of amendments to the Constitution called the 'Bill of Rights', which guarantees the following rights, among others:

The Second Amendment protects the right to own and carry guns

- the First Amendment guarantees freedom of speech
- the Second Amendment protects the right to carry guns
- the Fifth Amendment protects witnesses from being forced to incriminate themselves
- the 26th Amendment guarantees the right to vote

Regular, fair elections

Voters in the USA can vote for a whole range of elected officials at county, city, state and federal levels. These elected posts range from Prosecuting Attorneys at county level, to the Board of Governors of universities at state level up to members of Congress and the President at federal level.

At federal level there are major elections every 2 years. The Presidential elections happen in the same year as the elections for the House of Representatives and some of the Senate. In between Presidential elections there are 'midterm' elections, again involving all of the House of Representatives and one-third of the Senate.

Elections at federal level	
Post	**Elected**
President	Every 4 years.
The Senate	Senators are voted in for a 6-year term. One-third of seats are up for election every 2 years.
The House of Representatives	Every 2 years.

A free media not controlled by the government

In a famous film based on real events called 'All the President's Men', two journalists from the *Washington Post* discover a plot to cover up a break-in at the Democratic Party HQ in Watergate. The journalists claimed they had evidence that the cover up went all the way up to the Republican President at the time, President Richard Nixon. The film was a dramatisation of real events and the journalists, Bob Woodward and Carl Bernstein, published their story about the 'Watergate scandal' in the *Washington Post*. President Nixon eventually resigned from office, although it is likely that if he had not resigned, he would have been 'impeached', i.e. put on trial by Congress. This illustrates one of the very important functions of a free media in a democracy – to keep the citizens informed about the actions of their elected representatives.

There is a huge range of media in the United States, including around 15,000 radio stations, 1200 newspapers, 89% of the population are online and the government helps to fund the non–profit Public Broadcasting Service (PBS) and National Public Radio (NPR).

Washington Post journalists reported the 'Watergate Scandal'

Because of this, and because the First Amendment protects the right to freedom of speech, there is a very wide range of views expressed in the American media.

A choice between political parties

The two main political parties in the USA are the Democrats and the Republicans. This does not mean, however, that there is not a choice of political parties. For example, three other parties (The Libertarian Party, The Green Party and The Constitution Party) are described as 'The "Big Three" Third Parties', meaning that they will put up candidates at local, state and federal levels in a large number of states. There is also a whole range of smaller parties, including the America First Party, The Citizens Party of the United States and The Prohibition Party.

However, as was the case with India, there are some things that make America less democratic:

- in 2018, the press freedom organisation, Reporters Without Borders stated that the USA had fallen two places from 43 to 45 out of 180 countries. They said this was due to the 'Trump effect' caused by his 'media bashing' and referring to the 'fake media' who reported critical stories about him

- the last time a President did not come from the 'big two' was back in the middle of the 19th Century

- only the Democrats and the Republicans stand any chance of raising the huge amounts of money spent on election campaigns. In the Presidential election of 2016 the Democrats spent $768 million and the Republicans spent around $398 million

- as we will see later, certain groups in the USA, such as minorities and women, are under-represented in politics

Quick Test

1. Explain the importance of the Bill of Rights.

2. What evidence is there that the USA has 'regular elections'.

3. Describe the Watergate scandal and explain why it shows the importance of a free media.

4. What evidence is there both for and against the statement that American citizens have a wide choice of political parties.

The Importance of the USA in the world

Why should we study the USA?

For most of the second half of the 20th Century, the main world powers were the 'communist' Soviet Union and the 'capitalist' USA. These two 'superpowers' competed with each other in many different ways, including building up vast numbers of nuclear weapons. This rivalry was described as a 'Cold War'. However, since the collapse of Communism in Europe and the break-up of the Soviet Union, the United States is the world's only remaining superpower.

Why is the USA so powerful?

The economy of the USA
- The USA is the most technologically advanced economy in the world (but note: China is predicted to overtake the USA before 2020).
- The USA's Gross Domestic Product (i.e. the value of goods and services produced each year) is thought to be around 25% of the world's total.
- One-third of the world's entire trade takes place between the USA and the countries of the European Union.
- The USA is the UK's biggest single trading partner.
- The USA has for some time been the world's biggest exporter of food crops.

Because of the importance of the economy of the USA to the rest of the world, a downturn in the economy of the USA will affect economies around the world.

Military involvement
The USA has also played a major role in many of the conflicts throughout the world in the 20th and 21st Centuries, either as a member of NATO or the United Nations or on its own. In more recent times, the USA has played an important role in:

- **Afghanistan – Operation Enduring Freedom** – Following the 9/11 attack by al-Qaeda on the World Trade Center in New York, the USA led an invasion of Afghanistan, along with other countries such as the UK, aimed at destroying al-Qaeda in what was called 'The War on Terror'. Although Afghanistan's own military have taken over the main combat role, the USA still has over 15,000 troops in the country to support the Afghan forces.

- **Iraq – Operation Iraqi Freedom** – In March 2003 the USA and the UK invaded Iraq and brought down its leader Saddam Hussein, claiming that Iraq had stockpiles of 'weapons of

EXAM TIP

Military might – the USA is the most powerful military force in the world. It spends as much on weapons and defence as the rest of the world put together.

mass destruction'. No such stockpiles were found. After the setting up of a new government, the USA withdrew but sent troops back in 2014 to counter the Islamic State (IS) group. The Pentagon states that over 5000 US troops are still in Iraq.

- **Libya – UN Resolution 1973** – In March 2011 the United Nations passed a resolution approving 'all necessary measures' to stop the troops of Libyan leader Colonel Gaddafi killing Libyan civilians who were protesting against his government. The United States was one of several countries that took action to prevent these attacks. After the fall of the Gaddafi regime, a Government of National Accord was set up, but there have been ongoing conflicts between different groups including IS. At present the USA continues to target IS in air strikes inside Libya.

- **Syria** – In Syria, where a civil war is ongoing, the US has given support to groups rebelling against the Russian-backed Syrian President Bashar Assad. Although it has avoided direct conflict with Syrian troops, the USA has carried out air strikes against IS forces in Syria and launched cruise missiles against Syrian air bases in response to the use of chemical weapons.

American culture

- **Brands** – There are very few parts of the world where American brands are not present, from McDonald's to Burger King, Apple to Microsoft and Nike to Adidas. In fact, in 2018, four of the top five companies by 'brand value' were American: Amazon, Apple, Google and Facebook.

- **Cultural influences** – Some people think that American influences have led to the 'Americanisation' of their own cultures; the top five grossing films of all time were all produced by American film studios, although some, like the Harry Potter franchise, were made in the UK. Other 'blockbusters' seen by millions (if not billions) around the world have included films such as Avatar, Titanic and The Avengers. American companies also dominate the fast food industry. In the UK, the most popular fast food brands in 2018 were Subway and McDonald's – both American-owned companies.

Quick Test

1. Explain why the USA can be described as the world's last superpower.
2. Why is the economy of the USA so important to the rest of the world?
3. Describe the role the USA played in at least two recent conflicts.
4. What evidence is there to support those who are concerned about 'Americanisation'?

Population issues in the USA

Immigration

The topic of immigration, especially illegal immigration, is one that causes a great deal of discussion in the USA, especially among politicians. It regularly comes in the Top 5 of issues that concern American voters. During the 2016 Presidential election campaign, candidate Donald Trump promised that if he was elected he would 'build a wall' between the USA and Mexico to stop illegal immigration. The issue of 'illegal immigration' was one of the most significant in the election. In a CBS/YouGov poll in May of 2018, 51% agreed that a wall would be a 'good thing'.

The attraction of the USA

The USA has been the the top country in the world for immigrants for many years. In 2016 it took in 1,183,500 legal immigrants, more than any other country. Why is America so attractive to immigrants? Reasons for this can be divided into 'pull' factors – things that 'attract' people to the USA, and 'push' factors – things that 'force' people to leave their own countries.

Push factors

- **Poverty** – in 2018, Mexico was still the largest source of immigrants to the USA, followed by India and China. In 2017, Mexicans working in the USA earned six times more than they could at home in Mexico.
- **Conflict** – throughout the 20th Century, people came to the USA to escape conflicts in their own parts of the world. For example, the USA accepted over 800,000 people fleeing from countries like Vietnam, Cambodia and Laos.
- **Unemployment** – many of the Europeans who emigrated to America during the 19th and 20th Centuries did so to try to find work. Today, many Mexicans hope to find work in the USA.

Pull factors

- **Freedom** – rights and freedoms that many immigrants may not have had in their home country, e.g. the right to vote, freedom of worship, free speech.
- **Opportunity** – in the USA (the world's biggest capitalist country) it is relatively easy to start a new business. This attracts business people from other countries.
- **Family** – around two-thirds of legal immigrants come to the USA in order to join family members already living there.
- **Welfare** – the USA has a welfare system for poorer people and many states have a minimum wage. Washington DC has a minimum wage of $12.50 per hour in 2018.
- **The American Dream** is the idea that, no matter what your background, if you work hard in America you can become successful and have a very good life. This is very attractive to people who may live in poorer countries where there are not as many chances to get on in life.

The arguments for and against immigration

Because of the growing percentage of minorities compared with White people (it is likely that by the middle of the 21st Century Whites will account for less than half of the total population), the issue of immigration to the USA has been a controversial one in recent years.

Arguments for immigration:

- The USA was made successful and powerful by immigrants who today start up 25% of new businesses.
- Immigrants with special skills fill jobs where there is a skills gap.
- Immigration means there will be lots of young people in the future who will be able to work and pay taxes. Some countries like Russia have an ageing population.
- Immigrants bring new cultures to be enjoyed by everyone, e.g. food, music, etc.
- Immigrants are more law abiding. Native-born Americans are three times more likely to be in prison than legal immigrants.

Arguments against immigration:

- Immigrants often work for lower wages, which keeps wage levels low for other poorly paid workers.
- People in the existing population feel 'swamped' and threatened.
- Some studies have found that households headed by an immigrant are much more likely to rely on at least one welfare benefit compared with native households.
- Immigrants compete for low-paid, unskilled jobs, causing racial tension with other groups competing for the same jobs.
- Immigrants are often young and able-bodied. This means that the country they emigrate from loses many of its valuable workers.

Since being elected as President in 2016, Donald Trump has introduced several policies designed to control immigration. Immigration, particularly what he called 'illegal immigration', was at the centre of his campaign, with promises to build a wall along the US–Mexico border and make Mexico 'pay for it'. His policies since becoming President have included:

- Banning immigration from eight, mostly Muslim, countries.
- Cutting refugee numbers to their lowest level since 1980.
- Cancelling the Deferred Action for Childhood Arrivals (DACA) programme, which allowed adults who had arrived in the USA as the children of illegal immigrants to work and receive some benefits.
- A 'Zero Tolerance' approach to illegal immigration, involving prosecuting everyone who tried to cross the border with Mexico illegally.

Quick Test

1. Explain why the USA is so attractive to immigrants.
2. What is meant by 'push' and 'pull' factors?
3. Why are some people concerned about immigration?
4. In what ways has President Trump tried to reduce immigration to the USA?

Inequality in the USA

An equality gap

What are the reasons for continued inequality in the USA? Although the United States is the world's richest single country, there are groups of people who experience social, political and economic inequality. This equality 'gap' is most obvious when comparing Whites with other ethnic groups such as African-Americans and Hispanics, but it also applies to other groups, like women. Although the gap is getting narrower, there is still evidence of continuing inequality.

New York has almost 80,000 homeless people

Causes of social inequality

Education
- A good education greatly improves people's life chances.
- The quality of education in the USA varies greatly.
- Some can afford to go to private schools or well-off schools in the suburbs.
- Pupils in inner-city schools are more likely to drop out early.

Health
- The United States does not have a comprehensive government-provided health care system like the NHS in the UK.
- The government provides basic health insurance for the elderly (Medicare), the poor (Medicaid) and military veterans.
- Other people in the USA must buy health insurance or have it provided by their employer.
- President Obama's Affordable Care Act, known as 'Obamacare', in 2012 tried to increase the number of people with health insurance, but this has been reduced since the election of President Trump in 2016.
- In 2018, 12% of Americans had no health cover.
- Hispanic and Black people are less likely to have health insurance than Whites.

Housing
- Wealthier people will tend to live in the suburbs where the housing is of better quality.
- Suburbs are less likely to be affected by gangs, crime and drug abuse.
- Although poverty in the suburbs is increasing faster than in the cities, urban poverty is still twice as high.

Economic inequality

- **Discrimination** – people may face unfair treatment in employment because of such things as their race, gender and religion. Only three of the Fortune 500 companies in the USA have a black Chief Executive Officer (CEO).

- **Wealth** – the average standard of living in the USA is fairly high, but there are still large gaps between the rich and poor in the USA. In 2016, according to the US Census Bureau, 22% of black people lived below the poverty line, compared with 9% of white people.

- **Employment** – the levels of unemployment tend to be higher for certain groups, such as older women, minorities and people with few or no qualifications.

Unemployment, 2018			
Black	Hispanic	White	Overall
6.1%	4.5%	3.4%	3.8%

Bureau of Labor Statistics

Political inequality

There are fewer female and minority representatives in Congress than there should be according to their share of the population. Women, for example, make up over half of the US population but only 20% of members of Congress. Minorities make up 38% of the population but only 19% of members of Congress. Because of this, it is likely that issues affecting these groups are not discussed as much as they would be if there were more women and minorities in positions of power.

Bob Menendez,
a Hispanic Senator

Quick Test

1. Which groups in the USA are more likely to face social, political and economic inequality?
2. Explain the difference in the way health care is provided in the USA and the UK.
3. Which groups are less likely to have health cover?
4. 'Congress does not fully reflect the population of the USA.' What evidence is there to support this statement?

Flight from the cities

The White and middle class Black flight

In many of America's major cities, there are areas where the majority of the residents belong to a particular ethnic group. This separation comes about through choice as people separate themselves by moving away from mixed race areas. It may also be the result of poorer people, often minorities, not being able to afford to move to the more affluent suburbs.

The diagram below describes how this came about.

The White flight

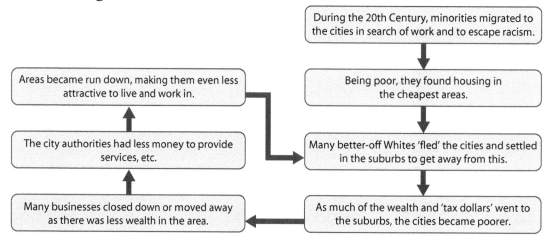

During the 20th Century, minorities migrated to the cities in search of work and to escape racism.

Being poor, they found housing in the cheapest areas.

Many better-off Whites 'fled' the cities and settled in the suburbs to get away from this.

As much of the wealth and 'tax dollars' went to the suburbs, the cities became poorer.

Areas became run down, making them even less attractive to live and work in.

The city authorities had less money to provide services, etc.

Many businesses closed down or moved away as there was less wealth in the area.

A model of US cities

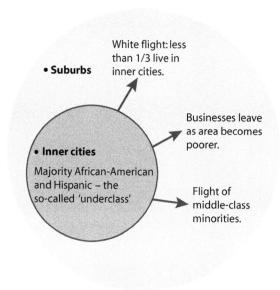

• Suburbs

White flight: less than 1/3 live in inner cities.

• Inner cities

Majority African-American and Hispanic – the so-called 'underclass'

Businesses leave as area becomes poorer.

Flight of middle-class minorities.

The underclass

As this population movement continues, the people 'left behind' in the inner cities – sometimes referred to as an 'underclass' – are more likely to be poor, unemployed, depending on welfare, affected by crime, drugs etc.

The circle of deprivation

Once in this position, it is very difficult for people to 'break out' as the diagram below explains.

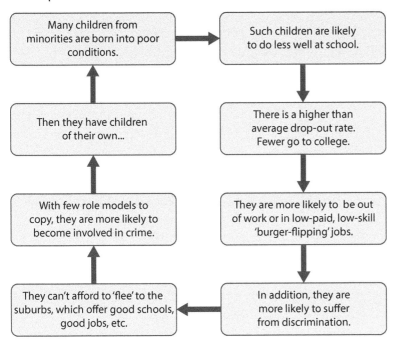

> **EXAM TIP**
>
> Flow diagrams like 'The White flight' are very good for showing 'links' between cause and effect. They are very useful for helping you to *explain* things – explaining will usually be worth more marks in the exam than just describing.

Diagram boxes:

- Many children from minorities are born into poor conditions.
- Such children are likely to do less well at school.
- There is a higher than average drop-out rate. Fewer go to college.
- They are more likely to be out of work or in low-paid, low-skill 'burger-flipping' jobs.
- In addition, they are more likely to suffer from discrimination.
- They can't afford to 'flee' to the suburbs, which offer good schools, good jobs, etc.
- With few role models to copy, they are more likely to become involved in crime.
- Then they have children of their own...

Quick Test

1. Describe the process that led to the growth of the so-called 'underclass' in some American cities.

2. Suggest three ways in which the circle of deprivation might be broken. Explain your suggestion.

Gender inequality in the USA

Are things getting better?

Evidence of increasing gender equality	Evidence of continuing gender inequality
Almost one-quarter of wives earn more than their husbands.	Women working full-time earn only 81% of the wage of full-time male workers.
Women make up 56% of US college students.	In 2018, the percentage of women in senior roles fell from 23% in the previous year to 21%.
The Pew Research Centre claims young women today will overtake average male earnings by 2020.	Over half of law school graduates are women, but they hold only 20% of senior posts.
Women now make up over 40% of graduates from the top Harvard Business School.	In 2018, only 24 of the Fortune 500 companies had a female CEO.
Women now make up 47% of the US workforce.	Men outnumber women two-to-one in jobs in science and engineering.

Reasons for this inequality

The evidence shows then that women are making progress, but equality still seems a long way off. There are many examples of successful and powerful women in business and politics, such as Mary Barra, the Chief Executive of General Motors, but only 50 out of the 400 richest people in the USA are women.

Elsewhere in this book you will read about the reasons why some women in the UK face inequality. The reasons that women in the USA face inequality are similar.

- **Glass ceiling** – there are far fewer women than men in top jobs, as though there is an invisible barrier, a 'glass ceiling', that prevents women getting to the top.
- **Family** – many women who take time out of their career to have a family can find it difficult to return to their job at the same level. Many women are also unable to take jobs that do not fit in with their childcare arrangements.
- **Prejudice** – some employers might discriminate against women because they think women cannot do particular jobs.
- **Maternity rights** – the Organisation for Economic Development and Cooperation (OECD) stated in 2016 that the USA was the only developed country whose government did not offer legally guaranteed paid maternity leave.
- **Gender gap** – the Global Gender Gap Report in 2017 stated that the USA was ranked only 49th out of 144 countries for gender equality.

> **EXAM TIP**
>
> When discussing gender inequality, remember that women from ethnic backgrounds tend to suffer even worse inequality than white women. For example, black women in the USA were on average paid 21% less than white women in 2018.

Mary Barra, head of America's largest car manufacturer

Women in American politics

As in other areas of life, women in the USA are making progress in politics; however, they are still a long way from equality. For example:

- there are currently a record three female Supreme Court judges out of nine; **however**, in its 229-year history, only four women justices have served on the Supreme Court
- the number of women elected to Congress has risen steadily; **however**, they made up only 19.3% of the Senate and 23% of the House of Representatives at the time this book was written
- three of the last five people to hold the very powerful post of Secretary of State in the USA have been female; **however**, they are the *only* three women who have ever held that post

Attempts to reduce inequality

The government of the USA has passed various laws and set up various organisations to try to reduce gender inequality.

- **The Federal Equal Pay Act 1963** – bans employers from paying women less than men for a job that requires a similar level of skill or responsibility.
- **Civil Rights Act 1964** – this made it illegal to refuse to hire someone or discriminate against them because of their race, colour or gender.
- **The Federal Family Medical Leave Act (FMLA) 1993** – allows 12 weeks of unpaid leave during a 12-month period for employees who need to care for a newborn, adopted, or foster child 1986 Supreme Court ruling - stated that sexual harassment in the workplace was illegal and discriminatory.
- **The Violence Against Women Act 1993** – provided funding to investigate and prosecute crimes of violence against women as well as setting up the Office on Violence Against Women
- **The Fair Pay Act 2009** – made it easier for women who were being paid unequally to take their employer to court.
- **The Minimum, Wage** – the Federal government in 2009 ruled that all states must pay a minimum wage of at least $7.80 per hour although many states pay more than this. This law affects women more than men because women make up 60% of low wage workers.

Quick Test

1. What evidence is there that 'women are making progress but equality still seems a long way off'?
2. Why can having children sometimes disadvantage women in work?
3. Describe the differences between male and female representation in Congress.
4. What attempts have been made to reduce gender inequality?

Participation of minorities

Minority groups in Congress

In the USA, some groups in the population participate in the political system less than others. There is also a difference in the levels of representation, especially at the federal level, although this has improved significantly in recent years. African-Americans make up 13.4% of the population but only just over 11% of the Congress. Hispanic people make up almost 17% of the population but only just over 10% of Congress.

Reasons for lower levels of participation: minority groups

Social reasons
- **Lower levels of education** – the more educated a person is, the more likely they are to understand political issues. Minorities often have lower levels of education.
- **Language and culture** – some groups speak English as a second language; politics is mostly reported in English by the media.
- **Living patterns** – minority groups are more likely to be concentrated in inner-city areas. Minority candidates are more likely to get elected at a local level. Across a whole state, however, they do not make up enough of the vote.
- **Crime** – in some states, convicted criminals lose their vote. A higher percentage of African-Americans are sent to prison than White people.

Economic reasons
- **Poverty** – people who are poor are much less likely to vote as they are more concerned with meeting their needs.
- **Unemployment** – people who suffer long-term unemployment feel 'left out' of society and may not see politics as relevant to them.

Political reasons
- **Role models** – people are more likely to vote if they see candidates like themselves. In the past there were fewer role models from minority groups.
- **Registration levels** – in the USA people are not allowed to vote unless they register to do so. Registration rates are usually lower among minority groups than Whites.
- **Loss of faith in politics** – some people who voted in the past may feel that it was not worthwhile because they still experience inequality and may stop voting.

EXAM TIP

Voter turnout is the phrase used to describe the percentage of the population that are entitled to vote and who actually do. In the last four Presidential elections, the turnout has increased steadily. Even then, however, the voter turnout in the 2016 election was only 58%.

Increasing minority participation

The Presidential election of 2008 saw increased voter turnout for African-Americans and Hispanics. In fact, the gap between Black and White voter numbers almost disappeared in the 2008 election. What are some of the reasons for this?

- Minority education attainment is increasing steadily. In 2018, 76% of Black and 79% of Hispanic people graduated from high school compared with 88% of White people.
- There are many more role models from minority groups, including former President Obama and US senators, such as Kamala Harris who represents California.
- There are many more TV channels broadcasting in minority languages.
- Voting campaigns that encourage people to vote are often targeted at minority groups, e.g. Operation Black Vote and Operation Voter Registration.
- TV campaigns 'backed' by celebrities encouraging minority groups to vote.
- Many states have made registering to vote easier, for example by introducing online registration and offering registration forms to people who are applying for driving licences, collecting benefits etc.

How important is the minority vote?

Traditionally, minority groups tend to support the Democratic Party. In the 2008 Presidential election, nearly all of the African-Americans who voted supported Obama (95%). Among Hispanic voters, 67% voted for Obama while 31% voted for the Republican candidate. In contrast, only 43% of White voters supported Obama. In the 2016 Presidential election, Black and Hispanic people did not vote for the Democratic candidate Hilary Clinton in the same numbers in which they voted for Obama, which according to some was the reason she lost the election.

The Congressional Black Caucus

This group, made up of the Black members of Congress, is becoming increasingly influential as more Black people get elected, especially to the House of Representatives. The aim of the CBC is to 'positively influence events that are relevant to African-Americans…'. In 2018, the CBC consisted of 46 members, with two in the Senate and 44 in the House of Representatives. All are members of the Democratic Party, although Republicans have been members in the past.

The importance of the Hispanic vote

Although Hispanics are under-represented and tend to participate less, they are becoming increasingly important: they are the fastest growing section of the US population and there are high concentrations of Hispanic voters in a number of so-called 'swing states', where Hispanic votes could decide who wins these states and in turn the Presidential election.

Quick Test

1. What evidence is there that some groups participate less than others?
2. Give one social, one political and one economic reason for lower participation.
3. Why is it especially important for the Democratic Party to make sure that minorities use their vote?
4. Explain why the Hispanic vote in 'swing states' could affect the result of a Presidential election.

Rights and responsibilities in the USA

In the section 'How democratic is the USA?' we saw that citizens of the USA have a very wide range of rights and that these rights are protected by the Constitution, especially in the Bill of Rights. However, rights cannot be enjoyed without responsibilities, for example if you have the right to own property then you have the responsibility to not steal the property of others.

Rights	Responsibilities
To vote for a large number of elected posts at various levels of government including county, state and federal.	• To use the vote. • To make an 'informed' choice – understand the issues and policies involved. • To accept the result of elections, even if they are not what you wanted.
Freedom of speech, including a free media.	• To not commit slander or libel against others. • To tell the truth. • To obey laws of secrecy and national security.
To take direct action, such as protesting and demonstrating.	• To act peacefully. • To stay within the law.
To join organisations such as trade unions, interest groups and political parties.	• To support these groups by activities such as fundraising and campaigning.
To bear arms (carry guns).	• To keep them secure and safe. • To use them only in self-defence or where permitted for sport. • To have the correct permissions to carry weapons.

EXAM TIP

The rights and responsibilities of people in the USA, with the exception of the right to bear arms, are very similar to those in other democracies such as the UK and India, so if you are asked a question about rights and responsibilities in one of your chosen democratic countries you can include the ones listed in the table above, as long as you give additional detail and relevant examples for that country of course.

How are these rights protected?

The rights described above and others are protected in a number of ways:

• They are part of the Constitution, which is the highest law in the land.
• There are courts at different levels up to and including the Supreme Court where people can take legal action if they feel their rights are being abused or threatened.
• The Supreme Court itself will declare an action or law 'unconstitutional' if it infringes these rights.
• The media will often bring attention to rights being abused or threatened.

The right to bear arms

The Second Amendment to the Constitution states that 'it is the right of the people to keep and bear (carry) arms'. This right has caused a great deal of discussion and debate, especially in recent years when America has suffered 'mass shootings'. Since 1999 alone, when two teenage pupils at Columbine High School shot dead 12 students and a teacher, there have been 10 other school shootings in which a total of 128 people have died. Gun facts:

- it is estimated that 47% of Americans own a gun
- there are approximately 270 million privately owned guns in America
- the USA has the highest level of private gun ownership in the world

Arguments for gun control as supported by the Brady Campaign:

- the *New England Journal of Medicine* states that guns kept at home for 'self-defence' are 43 times more likely to kill a family member or friend than an intruder
- according to the FBI, for every 'justifiable' hand gun killing, there are 50 hand gun murders
- approximately 3000 children are killed by guns in the USA each year according to a report in the *New York Times* in 2012

Arguments against gun control as supported by the National Rifle Association:

- the Constitution clearly states that the people of the USA have a right to keep and carry weapons
- guns are necessary for self-defence. If people are not allowed to keep guns then only criminals will have them as they will not obey the law
- banning guns will not prevent mass killings, as the people who commit these crimes will still be able to get guns illegally

Freedom of Speech

The First Amendment to the US Constitution protects freedom of speech, religion and the press. It also protects the right to peaceful protest. In recent years, there has been a lot of discussion about how far this freedom should be protected. Some people argue that it has gone too far and that some opinions are in fact 'hate speech'. Social media is often criticised for allowing such views to be expressed, but others argue that all opinions should be allowed to be expressed so that people can discuss them and put forward arguments for and against them to allow people to make up their own minds. The American Civil Liberties Union (ACLU), which is known for fighting for the rights of groups who have been discriminated against such as women and minorities, have even supported the right of white supremacist groups to hold a demonstration in Charlottesville in 2017.

Quick Test

1. Explain the phrase, 'rights cannot be enjoyed without responsibilities,' giving examples to support your answer

2. In what ways are the rights of US citizens 'protected'?

3. For either the Brady Campaign or the National Rifle Association, choose the two arguments that you think are the most convincing and explain why.

4. What arguments could be made for and against allowing people to express opinions that others might find 'extreme'?

Answers

Unit 1: Democracy in Scotland and the United Kingdom

The UK political system (page 25)

1. Separation of the powers works by giving each of the branches of government responsibility for certain powers so that no one branch has too much power.

2. The House of Commons is made up of 650 members elected using the First Past the Post System. The House of Lords is made up of Lords Spiritual and Lords Temporal. They are unelected.

3. The Monarch has no real power because most of the functions carried out by the monarch are ceremonial or are decided by the government of the day.

4. Devolution means that certain powers have been transferred from the UK Parliament to the other decision making bodies in Northern Ireland, Scotland and Wales.

Participating in a representative democracy (page 27)

1. In a representative democracy, the people will choose or elect representatives who will in turn make decisions and laws which will apply to the people.

2. The main features of a democracy are guaranteed rights, regular, free and fair elections, a free media and a genuine choice between political parties.

3. Scotland and the UK are democratic: they have all of the features described in answer 2.

4. The answer to this question will vary depending on your choice. Make sure you have given a clear reason for saying why you think it is the most important.

The Government of Scotland (page 29)

1. The First Minister is the leader of the largest party and is responsible for choosing the Cabinet, representing Scotland in its dealings with the UK and the rest of the world and has overall responsibility for the policies of the Scottish Government.

2. The Scottish Parliament can hold the Scottish Government to account through Question Time, committees and debates.

3. The Scottish Parliament also passes laws and represents the views of the Scottish People.

4. The answer to this question will vary depending on your choice. Make sure you have given a clear reason for saying why you think it is the most important.

Scotland's voting system (page 31)

1. It is important for voters in a democracy to use their vote because it shows how they feel about how well the government is doing, it allows the peaceful changeover of governments and it makes governments accountable to the people.

2. The First Past the Post system can be said to be unfair because constituencies are often won with less than half the votes and some parties with a more 'spread out' support get far fewer seats.

3. Coalition government can have a broader range of views in it but it might give a lot of power to a small party.

Scottish independence (page 33)

1. The three different viewpoints about Scottish independence are that supporters of independence believe Scotland would be better off, while those who oppose independence believe that Scotland is better off as part of the UK. The third view is that Scotland should remain in the UK but have more powers.

2. The answer to this question will vary depending on your choice. Make sure you include the key ideas in your summary.

3. The answer to this question will vary depending on your choice. Make sure you include the key ideas in your summary.

Election campaigns (page 35)

1. The main difference between the way newspapers and the broadcast media report on politics is that the broadcast media must remain neutral whereas newspapers will often support a particular political party.

2. The answer to this question will vary depending on your choice. Make sure you have given a clear reason for saying why you think they are effective.

3. This is your opinion, there is no right or wrong answer but, as always, you must give reasons.

4. The main role of social media during election campaigns is to get the message of the parties across to as many people as possible in the hope of persuading them to vote for the party. It is also used to 'target' messages to groups and areas the party thinks it might gain support from.

The work of an MSP (page 37)

1. Within their constituencies or regions, MSPs can act on behalf of the people they represent by attending events and meetings to hear points of view, contact officials etc on their behalf and hold regular surgeries. (You could also mention contacting other elected representatives and supporting local campaigns.)

2. The answer to this question will vary depending on your choice. Make sure you have given clear reasons for saying why you think your chosen methods are most effective.

3. Committees are a small group of MSPs who scrutinise the work of different parts of the government, carry out enquiries and look closely at new bills.

Political parties (page 39)

1. The main purposes of political parties are to get as many of their candidates as possible elected to bodies such as local councils and parliaments in Scotland, the UK and Europe. They also represent the views of their members.

2. In the Scottish election of 2016 the SNP were the single largest party followed by the Conservatives and then Labour. In the UK elections the Conservatives were the biggest single party followed by Labour and the SNP. The similarity between the two is that the biggest party did not have more than half of the total seats.

3. A manifesto is a list of the policies a political party will put forward in the election.

4. This is your opinion, there is no right or wrong answer but, as always, you must give reasons.

Pressure groups (page 41)

1. Pressure groups are organisations of people who share common goals. They try to influence decision making to get something they want.

2. A sectional group tries to protect the interests of a group or 'section' of people whereas a cause group, or promotional group, promote a cause scuch as the environment.

3. An insider group will have closer links with decision makers and will often be asked for their advice or opinions whereas an outsider group will not have the same links and will often put pressure on decision makers.

4. This is your opinion, there is no right or wrong answer but, as always, you must give reasons. Look carefully at the list of advantaged and disadvantages to help you.

Trade unions (page 43)

1. A trade union is an organisation of workers and their main aim is to improve and protect the working conditions of their members in the workplace.

2. A shop steward represents the views of the workforce to the management and will negotiate with management on behalf of their members. Shop stewards also act as a link between the union organisation and the union members in the workplace.

3. Members can take part in the work of the union by attending meetings, standing for a union post, voting in union elections, taking part in industrial action and paying fees to the union.

4. This is your decision – there is no right or wrong answer but, as always, you must give reasons.

Unit 2: Social Issues in the United Kingdom

Poverty and social exclusion in the UK (page 45)

1. Relative poverty is when some people in a society have a lower than average income whereas absolute poverty is when someone is not able to meet their basic human needs.

2. The cycle of social exclusion describes how some people are socially excluded by a combination of poor housing, family breakdown, bad health etc. These problems are very often connected so that poor health is much more common in poor areas.

3. The groups more likely to be affected by social exclusion are the elderly, ethnic minorities, women, lone parent families and people with physical and mental needs.

4. The Scottish government's figures for poverty in Scotland show that the following groups are more likely to be affected by poverty and social exclusion: single adult women, minority ethnic groups, children and pensioners.

The causes of poverty (page 47)

1. The National Living Wage is the amount set by the government that employers must pay their workers is they are over a certain age. The "real living wage" is a higher amount that organisations such as The Living Wage Foundation say *should* be paid.

2. The Joseph Rowntree Foundation report showed that the top three reasons for escaping poverty involved getting a job or a better job.

3. The families most likely to have a low income are lone parent families, reconstituted families and families which have the following: no adult in employment; headed by a teenage parent; children under five; a disabled child; a large number of children.

4. Some areas are poorer than others because of high unemployment, poor education, and higher levels of sickness, crime and drug abuse.

The effects of poverty (page 49)

1. Children born into poorer households are more likely to have problems from birth, die earlier and miss more school.

2. Fewer pupils from poorer backgrounds gain a place at university as they are less likely to come from households that encourage learning, more likely to miss school due to poor health and more likely to attend schools in areas of multiple deprivation where they are less likely to get the grades needed to get in to university.

3. The kinds of problems facing Scotland's poorest areas include fewer jobs, lack of role models, substance misuse, anti social behaviour and lack of amenities.

4. The connection between poverty and addiction is that poorer people are much more likely to suffer addiction to drugs and alcohol.

Tackling poverty: 1 (page 51)

1. A welfare state provides a range of benefits to help people when they are unemployed, sick or have a low income.

2. This is your opinion, there is no right or wrong answers but, as always, you must give reasons.

3. The phrase "welfare to work" means to help and encourage people who depend on welfare benefits to find employment through various government schemes.

4. Some volunteers will get together in local Work Clubs, carry out voluntary work and help people to start their own business.

Tackling poverty: 2 (page 53)

1. The main aims of The Fairer Scotland Action plan are a fairer Scotland for all, ending child poverty, a strong start for all young people, fairer working lives and improving the lives for older people.

2. Scottish Enterprise and Highlands and Islands Enterprise try to create jobs by giving business advice, help with skills training, developing products and helping to find premises.

3. More Choices More Chances shows the importance of education in tackling poverty.

4. Free Early Education and Childcare might reduce poverty and inequality by allowing parents more opportunities to work and by improving the life chances of disadvantaged and vulnerable children.

Health inequality (page 55)

1. Apart from poverty, the other factors which can influence health are age, gender, area, ethnic group and genetic factors.

2. The name sometimes given to Scotland is 'The Sick Man of Europe'.

3. The main aims of "Fairer Healthier Scotland" are to increase physical activity, improve mental wellbeing and to reduce premature mortality, smoking, alcohol related hospital admissions and drug use.

4. The policies which show the importance of focusing on young people are Hungry for Success and free school meals.

Ethnic inequality (page 57)

1. It can be said that Scotland was and is a multicultural nation because historically Scotland was made up of people from many different groups and today people of Black Minority and Ethnic origin make up just over 2% of Scotland's population.

2. The evidence that there is BAME group inequality is that they tend to have higher rates of poverty, unemployment, criminal convictions and poor health. They also tend to have lower wages, educational attainment and fewer promoted jobs and are more likely to be stopped, searched and arrested.

3. The main reasons for this inequality are that BME groups are more likely to live in poorer areas of cities, have English as a second language, have less education and are more likely to suffer from prejudice and discrimination.

4. The main point of the Equality Act is to prevent discrimination against people as a result of factors such as age, race, gender, sexual orientation and status of relationship.

Ethnic inequality: employment (page 59)

1. The appointment of Tidjanie Thiam can be described as 'unusual' because he was the first Black CEO of one of Britain's top 100 companies.

2. The evidence that BME groups face greater employment inequality might include: twice as many young black males are unemployed than white; BME groups make up 10.3% of the population but only 6.3% of managers; the average level of employment for BME groups is well below that of whites.

3. The evidence that some BME groups face greater inequality than others is that Pakistani and Bangladeshi origin groups are more likely to suffer worse health and earn less than other BME groups such as Indian and Chinese.

4. Reasons for continued inequality include: more likely to live in deprived areas, fewer job opportunities, English as a second language and 'unwelcoming' professions.

Ethnic inequality: health (page 61)

1. The main factor that has the biggest impact on health inequality among BME groups is poverty and social exclusion.

2. The evidence that some ethnic groups have worse health than others is that over 14% of people of Pakistani and Bangladeshi origin are 'not in good health' which is the highest percentage of all the BEM groups shown.

3. Black-Caribbean and African people are more likely to come in to contact with mental health services because they are more likely be referred by the prison and court system.

4. The attempts which have been made to tackle health inequalities include the Equality Act, Race for Health, Equally Well and NHS Scotland Equality Outcomes (your answer should include the main points of each of these policies).

Gender inequality: employment (page 63)

1. Evidence of progress might include: record number of MPs, increased number of board members, increasing educational success and a falling wage gap. Evidence of continued inequality might include: average pay gap still around 15%, lower % in top jobs, small numbers in the Cabinet.

2. The main reason why so many women are in part time jobs is because of the need for childcare.

3. The 'glass ceiling' refers to an 'invisible' barrier which seems to stop many women from reaching top posts.

Gender inequality: health (page 65)

1. The evidence of gender health inequality might include: higher suicide rates among men, higher rates of illness & depression among women and higher rates of cancer among men.

2. Occupation is more likely to affect the health of men because men are more likely to work in dangerous conditions, use heavy equipment and power tools and come into contact with dangerous substances.

3. 'Risky activities' include such things as driving fast, taking part in dangerous sports and getting involved in violence.

4. Biology can affect health because certain diseases are much more likely to affect one gender or another, for example prostate and breast cancers. It might also be the case that women have more biological protection from disease than men.

Unit 3: International Issues – China

The Government of China (page 67)

1. The CPC controls what people are allowed to read, watch and say; they control all aspects of the school curriculum and they control the number of children people are allowed to have.

2. The CPC controls the government because at all levels, the government is run by CPC members including the top posts such as the Presidency and Prime Minister.

3. The CPC membership is mostly male, drawn from certain occupations and new members must be nominated by an existing party member and undergo lots of background checks.

4. The Standing Committee of the Politburo takes all of the most important decisions affecting the country. It also decides who will get the top jobs in the government and the Party.

How democratic is China? (page 69)

1. In the village of Wukan in 2012, a local village elder Lin Zuluan, was voted village chief in what many described as a free and fair election however, in 2016 Lin Zuluan was arrested and several villagers were given long prison sentences for protesting against his arrest.

2. There is no genuine choice between political parties in China because only the CPC stands at national level and any smaller parties are expected to 'follow the direction' of the CPC.

3. Amnesty have criticised China's record on human rights because it has the largest number of imprisoned journalists in the world and overuses the death penalty.

4. The Law on Guarding State Secrets is deliberately vague so that it can be applied to anything.

The importance of China in the world (page 71)

1. The increased number of middle class people in China might benefit the West because many of the goods they are buying are made in the West.

2. The growth of China might lead to increased environmental damage and increasing prices for the rest of the world as China 'buys up' the resources it needs.

3. China is increasingly important to Scotland because of the growing demand for Scottish goods especially in things such as whisky and foods.

4. The phrase "anti-access / area denial" describes Chinas aim to become the main power in important areas of Asia and the Pacific. is Chinas plan to invest billions of dollars in infrastructure to link China with countries in Asia, Africa and Europe.

Population issues in China (page 73)

1. Before 2015, China enforced a 'one child policy' to try to control the growth of its population but this led to a rapidly falling birth-rate, fears of an ageing population and a possible shortage of workers in the future. The Chinese government is now offering incentives to women to encourage them to have more children.

2. The 4-2-1 family means that a single person might have to look after 2 parents and 4 grandparents.

3. There is gender imbalance because people have been choosing to have boys rather than girls and this will mean that there will be more men than women of marriageable age and a growth in 'bride trafficking'.

4. As a result of an ageing population, China will have to spend more on benefits for the elderly, people will have to work longer and overcrowding in the cities will increase.

Inequality in education (page 75)

1. The Gaokoa exam is the very tough annual exam that decides whether or not students will get in to a good university.

2. Many children do not get a good education because children living in rural areas drop out of school earlier, cannot pay the extra fees for books etc., and are likely to have a poorer standard of education as it is difficult to get the best teachers to work in rural areas.

3. The evidence of success of the Chinese education system might include: higher PISA scores than for many Western countries, increasing numbers of science, technology engineering and maths graduates and falling levels of illiteracy.

4. The Chinese government is concerned about the style of learning in schools because it relies too much on memorisation and not enough on creative and imaginative thinking skills.

Wealth inequality (page 77)

1. The comment by Yu Hua describes the increasing inequality between the rich and poor in China.

2. The Government has tried to reduce inequality by building low-cost homes, increasing the minimum wage and giving more help to rural areas.

3. The evidence that China is reducing inequality might include: 600 million out of poverty since 1981, 70% said they were better off than 5 years ago and 92% said they had a better standard of living than their parents.

4. The Hukou system means that each person 'belongs' to a certain area and if they move out of the area they can lose certain rights. This means that many migrant workers have to work for less, lose benefits such as health care and education live in poor conditions.

Inequality: women in China (page 79)

1. The evidence that women are under-represented in politics might include: very few women ever make it in to the Politburo, get elected as the head of Provinces or get elected as village leaders.

2. The move away from smoke stack industries will benefit women as there will be more opportunities and less discrimination in the new industries such as the service industry.

3. The 'traditional' role of women 'forces' them to be carers both for their own children and elderly relatives often including the husband's parents.

4. The Chinese Government has encouraged greater employment of women, improved benefits for working women, introduced quotas for some jobs and passed laws about sexual harassment.

Tackling inequality in China (page 81)

1. The 13th Five Year Plan aims to reduce inequality by making it as important a target as improving the economy. The Plan is also encouraging new industries in rural areas, reducing the gap between living standards in urban and rural areas. A Health Action Plan has been introduced to improve health care for all and children are to get a basic education to improve job chances. Elderly people will get improved benefits and millions of low cost houses are to be built.

> 2. The minimum wage is paid by employers and should be at least enough to guarantee workers can meet their everyday needs. Some states can afford to pay a higher level than others but some workers complain that wages do not keep up with prices and that many employers just take more money off their workers' wages to pay for the increase.
>
> 3. Tackling inequality in:
>
>   a. Health: spending $1trillion by 2020, health insurance for 95% of population.
>
>   b. Housing: houses built for Olympics sold at affordable prices, millions of low cost houses planned.
>
>   c. Employment: minimum wage job creation, back to work schemes for unemployed.

Unit 3: International Issues – India

Government of India: 1 (page 83)

1. A federal government means there is a central government for the whole country and separate state governments for each state. In India the central government is called the Union Government and each of the 28 states has its own government although the Union Government can 'over-rule' the states.

2. The Parliament and President make new laws and change existing ones; the Prime Minister and the Council of Ministers make decisions about the day-to-day running of the country; the Supreme Court makes sure the law is upheld and enforced.

3. Both the Indian and the UK governments have two houses, an elected Prime Minister and separation of the powers.

Government of India: 2 (page 85)

1. Checks and balances means that each branch of the government can amend or veto the acts of another so that no one branch can become too powerful.

2. The answer to this question will vary depending on your choice. Make sure you have given a clear reason for saying why you think it is the most important.

3. The evidence that 'the role of President in India carries no real power' is that the President can only act on the advice of the Prime Minister and the role of President is largely ceremonial.

How democratic is India? (page 87)

1. You would decide how democratic a country is by 'measuring it' against the key features of a democracy including regular, free and fair elections, a free media, genuine choice of parties and guaranteed rights.

2. Women, poor people and members of lower castes do not always receive the rights they are supposed to.

3. A free media is important in a democracy because it keeps the people informed, acts as a 'watchdog' on the government and allows people to express their views.

4. India is ranked so low in the World Press Freedom Index due to the high percentage of the media controlled by people from upper castes, the killing of journalists and increasing restrictions on press freedom.

India's importance in the world (page 89)

1. We should study India because of its growing economic and international power, its importance to Scotland and the UK and the fact that it is one of the world's nuclear powers.

2. The evidence that India's economy is becoming more important to the world might include: it is a G20 member, it will be ranked 9th by 2017, it is the fourth largest purchaser in the world and half of the world's 'back office' is in India.

3. The Scottish Government is trying to encourage stronger links with India to benefit from a growing demand in India for luxury products from Scotland and to encourage students from India to study in Scotland.

4. The purpose of the so-called 'quad of democracies' is to counter growing Chinese influence in South East Asia.

Population issues in India (page 91)

1. Six key words to sum up the population of India might include: young, mixed, moving, growing, urbanising and crowded.

2. The problems caused by the growing population include: pressure on natural resources, overcrowded and unhealthy cities, environmental damage and growing demand for education, health care, houses and jobs.

3. Some people have more children than others because the children can work in poorer families, there is a high child death rate and some people will have less access to birth control than others.

Population issues in India: the move to the cities (page 93)

1. Urbanisation means people leave the countryside and move to the towns and cities.

2. Many people in rural India are finding it hard to meet their needs because it is getting harder to make a living, many farmers are in debt and the changeover to cash crops is expensive and many farmers can't afford this.

3. The other reasons for urbanisation include: more jobs, better paid jobs, better services and cultural attractions.

4. Urbanisation causes problems including poor sanitation, water shortages, and the growth of slums.

Inequality: education in India (page 95)

1. The evidence that India is not doing as well as it should be in education is shown in the OECD report showing that compared to similar countries India has fewer in higher education, poorer graduate employability and lower standards of literacy.

2. The reasons for this might include: some states are richer than others and can provide better education, the caste system and gender prejudice and some people can afford to buy a better education than others.

3. The evidence that policies to improve education are having some success is that 90% complete primary education, increased numbers of schools, teachers and universities and a falling gap between male and female school enrolment.

Inequality: the caste system (page 97)

1. The caste system divided the population into groups or castes. A person born into a poor caste remains within that caste for the rest of their lives.

2. The caste system affects people's lives because lower castes often have lower wages, poorer education, lack of property and poorer living and health standards.

3. The government has tried to reduce the impact of the caste system by passing several laws which try to outlaw caste discrimination, help lower castes to set up businesses and setting aside a certain number of jobs for people from lower castes.

Inequality: women and girls (page 99)

1. The evidence that it is possible for some women to become successful is that they have reached powerful positions in politics and business such as the leaders of political parties and the Speaker of the Lok Sabha.

2. India is ranked as the worst place in the G20 to be female because of things such as sex selective abortions, traditional views about female 'inferiority', the dowry system and adolescent marriage.

3. The Indian Government has tried to tackle gender inequality by including female rights in the Constitution, protecting women's right to own property and passing laws to protect women and girls from violence.

Unit 3: International Issues – The USA

The Government of the USA: 1 (page 101)

1. Separation of the powers works by giving each of the branches of government responsibility for certain powers so that no one branch has too much power (see similar question in 'The UK political system – an overview'). Checks and balances means that each branch can limit and control the power of the other two.

2. Both the Indian and the US political systems have separation of the powers, checks and balances, two elected houses and an elected President.

The Government of the USA: 2 (page 103)

1. The Supreme Court can have a big influence on people's lives because it is the final court of appeal, it protects the constitution and its decisions can bring about large changes such as the desegregation of education.

2. The appointment of the next Supreme Court Judge to fill the vacancy might 'tip the balance' of opinion in the Court because at the time this book was written there were four judges who had been appointed by a Democratic President and four by a Republican President. Presidents usually pick judges who have similar views to themselves.

3. The evidence that the President plays a part in each of the powers is that he appoints Supreme Court judges, he can propose new laws and he can change or veto laws passed by Congress.

How democratic is the USA? (page 105)

1. The Bill of Rights is important because it guarantees many important rights such as freedom of speech, the right not to incriminate yourself and the right to vote.

2. The evidence that the USA has 'regular elections' is that it has a very wide range of elections which take place very frequently at all levels of government from local to Federal.

3. The Watergate scandal was caused when the President at the time tried to 'cover up' a break-in at a rival party's HQ. It shows the importance of a free media because the *Washington Post* brought the story to public attention.

4. The evidence that American citizens have a wide choice of political parties is that there are a number of parties which contest elections at various levels. The evidence against is that only the Democrats or Republicans stand any chance of winning.

The importance of the USA in the world (page 107)

1. The USA can be described as the world's last superpower because the other previous 'superpower', the USSR, has broken up and no longer exists.

2. The economy of the USA is so important to the world because it makes about 25% of all goods and services in the world, one-third of the world's trade is between the USA and the European Union and the USA is the world's biggest supplier of important crops.

3. The role played by the USA in recent conflicts: Afghanistan: by far the largest number of troops involved in Operation Enduring Freedom; Iraq: Invaded Iraq in search of weapons of mass destruction but were found; Libya: used its air power and drones to attack Libyan aircraft and prevent attacks on the Libyan people.

4. The evidence to support those who are concerned about Americanisation is that American brands and cultural influences have spread to most parts of the world.

Population issues in the USA (page 109)

1. The USA is attractive to immigrants because of the freedoms that the USA has, the opportunities of the American Dream, a welfare system and jobs.

2. Push factors cause people to want to leave their own country to 'escape' things like conflict and bad government whereas 'pull factors' attract people to places like the USA and they include the things listed in the answer above.

3. Some people are concerned about immigration because they believe immigrants work for lower wages, some people feel 'swamped', others believe immigrants rely too much on welfare and it can cause racial tension.

4. President Trump has tried to reduce immigration to the USA by banning immigration from some countries, cutting refugee numbers, cancelling the Deferred Action for Childhood Arrivals and a 'zero tolerance' approach to illegal immigration.

Inequality in the USA (page 111)

1. The groups in the USA that are more likely to face inequality are African-Americans, Hispanics, other minorities and women.

2. In the UK health care is provided for all by the NHS which is funded by the government whereas in the USA, the government provides basic health insurance for the elderly, the poor and military veterans while other people must buy health insurance cover or have it provided by their employer.

3. Hispanics and Black people are less likely to have health cover than other groups.

4. The evidence that Congress does not fully reflect the population of the USA is that women make up over half the population of the USA but only 20% of Congress while minorities make up 38% of the population but only 19% of Congress.

Answers

Flight from the cities (page 113)

1. The underclass developed as people who were able to move away to better areas did so, leaving behind those people who were less likely to have the skills and education to move away, creating an underclass.

2. The answer will depend on your suggestion. Be careful! No matter how good you think your suggestion might be, remember it has to be paid for and most Americans don't like the idea of increased taxation!

Gender inequality in the USA (page 115)

1. The evidence that women are making progress is that they are earning more than in the past, getting more education and more jobs. However, there is still a wage gap, and there are far fewer women than men in top jobs.

2. Having children can sometimes be a disadvantage to women in work because they may have to take a career break and they may have to take jobs to fit in with childcare arrangements.

3. When this book was written, women made up only 17% of the Senate and 21% of the House of Representatives.

4. The attempts to reduce this inequality includes passing a range of laws which are meant to prevent unequal pay, job discrimination, discrimination in education and promote equal opportunities.

Participation of minorities (page 117)

1. The evidence that some groups participate less than others is that women, African-Americans and Latinos are all underrepresented in Congress compared to their share of the population.

2. This answer will depend on the reason you chose. Remember you MUST use your own words.

3. It is especially important for the Democratic Party to make sure that minorities use their vote because in the last Presidential election nearly all African-Americans and over two-thirds of Hispanic people voted for the Democratic President Obama.

4. The Hispanic vote in 'swing states' could affect the result of a Presidential election because they are the fastest growing section of the population and there are high concentrations of Hispanics in some of these 'swing states'.

Rights and responsibilities in the USA (page 119)

1. The phrase means that in order to enjoy rights, people must respect the rights of others. An example might be the right to carry guns carries with it the responsibility to store and use them safely.

2. The rights of US citizens are protected by the Constitution, the courts and the media.

3. This answer will depend on which group you choose. Remember, you must explain WHY you think the arguments are convincing.

4. The arguments for allowing people to express views that other might find 'extreme' are that the US Constitution protects freedom of speech and that all opinions should be allowed to be expressed so that arguments for and against them can be heard to allow people to make up their own minds. Others argument that some views have gone 'too far; and are in fact hate speech.